UNDERSTANDING
KURT VONNEGUT

Understanding Contemporary
American Literature

Matthew J. Bruccoli, *Editor*

UNDERSTANDING
Kurt
VONNEGUT

by WILLIAM RODNEY ALLEN

THE UNIVERSITY OF SOUTH CAROLINA PRESS

© 1991 University of South Carolina

Cloth edition published by the University of South Carolina Press, 1991
Paperback edition published in Columbia, South Carolina,
by the University of South Carolina Press, 2009

www.sc.edu/uscpress

Manufactured in the United States of America

18 17 16 15 14 13 12 11 10 09   10 9 8 7 6 5 4 3 2 1

The Library of Congress has cataloged the cloth edition as follows:
Allen, William Rodney.
    Understanding Kurt Vonnegut / by William Rodney Allen.
        p. cm. — (Understanding contemporary American literature)
    Includes bibliographical references (p.) and index.
    ISBN 0-87249-722-4
    1. Vonnegut, Kurt—Criticism and interpretation. I. Title. II. Series.
PS3572.O5Z53   1990
813'.54—dc20   90-12831

ISBN: 978-1-57003-886-0 (pbk)

for Paul Smith

CONTENTS

EDITOR'S PREFACE

Understanding Contemporary American Literature has been planned as a series of guides or companions for students as well as good nonacademic readers. The editor and publisher perceive a need for these volumes because much of the influential contemporary literature makes special demands. Uninitiated readers encounter difficulty in approaching works that depart from the traditional forms and techniques of prose and poetry. Literature relies on conventions, but the conventions keep evolving; new writers form their own conventions—which in time may become familiar. Put simply, *UCAL* provides instruction in how to read certain contemporary writers—identifying and explicating their material, themes, use of language, point of view, structures, symbolism, and responses to experience.

The word *understanding* in the series title was deliberately chosen. Many willing readers lack an adequate understanding of how contemporary literature works; that is, what the author is attempting to express and the means by which it is conveyed. Although the criticism and analysis in the series have been aimed at a level of general accessibility, these introductory volumes are meant to be applied in conjunction with the works they cover. Thus they do not provide a substitute for the works and authors they introduce, but rather prepare the reader for more profitable literary experiences.

M. J. B.

ACKNOWLEDGMENTS

I would like to thank several people who helped make this book possible. Jan Samet and Flemming Thomas at the Northwestern State University Library were indispensable to my work. Among my colleagues at the Louisiana School for Math, Science and the Arts, I must mention Drs. Nahla Beier, Fraser Snowden, Allen Tubbs, and Art Williams as essential sources of insight and inspiration. My research assistant, Megan O'Neil, tracked down references, proofed the manuscript, offered editorial advice—all with an extraordinary cheerfulness and care. I'm very much in her debt.

Most of all I thank, and am thankful for, Cindy, Emily, and Claire—who confirm Vonnegut's recognition in *Bluebeard* that "Now it's the women's turn."

UNDERSTANDING
KURT VONNEGUT

CHAPTER ONE

Understanding Kurt Vonnegut

Career

Kurt Vonnegut's career has been one of the more interesting ones in American literary history. In the forty years since he published his first short story in 1950, Vonnegut has experienced a virtual roller coaster ride of literary reputation—from obscurity to international fame to being dismissed by critics as a mere "popular" writer to regaining some critical respect for his most recent work. Beginning as a science fiction writer, he produced two undistinguished novels in that genre in the 1950s before finding his distinctive voice in four innovative fictions of the 1960s—*Mother Night* (1962), *Cat's Cradle* (1963), *God Bless You, Mr. Rosewater* (1965), and his masterpiece, *Slaughterhouse-Five* (1969). In the middle 1970s, however, two weak novels and a backlash against his enormous popularity led to a reversal in his reputation, at least among "serious" readers. In the 1980s, with the publication of *Jailbird* (1979), *Deadeye Dick* (1982), *Galápagos* (1985), and *Bluebeard*

(1987), Vonnegut made a quiet but undeniable come-back with academic readers, while retaining a healthy portion of his popular following. By the age of sixty-five Vonnegut had produced twelve novels, a collection of short stories, a Broadway play, and two collections of essays. Regardless of what he writes in the future or how critics view his other work, *Slaughterhouse-Five* will almost certainly win Vonnegut a permanent place in American literature.

Kurt Vonnegut, Jr., was born on November 11, 1922, in Indianapolis, Indiana, a city he would use again and again in his novels as a symbol of American middle-class values. Jerome Klinkowitz, a leading critic of Von-negut's fiction, has written that "the key to Vonnegut's genius . . . is his unique ability to fashion a work of art out of ordinary middle class life."[1] The Vonneguts were hardly middle class in the late 1920s; Kurt Sr. was one of the most prominent architects in the city, and his wife, Edith, was the daughter of a wealthy Indianapolis brewer. But five years later the cessation of building in the Depression cut so sharply into their income that they had to sell their lavish home, move to a more mod-est neighborhood, and take Kurt Jr. out of private school. This radical change in economic circumstances traumatized his parents: Vonnegut's father thereafter virtually gave up on life, and his mother literally did so in 1944, when she died of an overdose of sleeping pills. Kurt Jr.'s lifelong pessimism clearly has its roots in his parents' despairing response to the Depression. As he confessed in an interview, "I learned a bone-deep sadness from them."[2]

At his new school, Shortridge High, Vonnegut made the best of things, writing for the school newspaper, the *Echo*. At Cornell University, though a chemistry major, he continued his journalistic work, becoming managing editor of the student paper, the *Sun*. Like Hemingway before him, Vonnegut would be influenced all his life as a writer by the simple rules of journalism: get the facts right; compose straightforward, declarative sentences; know your audience. Both his realistic fiction of the 1980s and collections of nonfiction, (*Wampeters, Foma and Granfalloons* [1974] and *Palm Sunday* [1981]) suggest the enduring effect of his early newspaper experience.

When World War II broke out, Vonnegut was sixteen years old; at the age of twenty he enlisted in the army and was sent to Europe, where he was captured by the Germans in the Battle of the Bulge on December 22, 1944. Less than two months later he experienced the event that would profoundly affect the rest of his life: as he puts it, "I was present in the greatest massacre in European history, which was the destruction of Dresden by fire-bombing."[3] On February 13, 1945, American and British bombers destroyed Dresden, a city on the Elbe River in what is now East Germany, by dropping high explosives followed by incendiary bombs, which turned the nonmilitarized city into an inferno that killed at least 130,000 people. Vonnegut and a few fellow prisoners and their guards survived only because they were quartered in a meat locker sixty feet below ground. For weeks after the attack Vonnegut was on a work detail whose job was to burn what was left of thousands of the dead.

After the war, like many returning veterans, Vonnegut quickly married, had children, and was faced with the responsibility of supporting his family. After dropping out of the graduate program in anthropology at the University of Chicago (he would later receive his MA from Chicago, which accepted *Cat's Cradle* as his thesis), he moved to Schenectady, New York, to take a job as a publicist for the General Electric Corporation. Vonnegut, however, was far from content with his job as a booster for the corporate world. As Richard Giannone describes Vonnegut's jaundiced view of GE, "Profit motives, he saw, were couched as sentimental tributes to pure science; individual freedom was sacrificed for professional advancement; and research was conducted without regard for its necessity or desirability. He saw that technology was developed in a moral vacuum."[4] The scientific research that had produced nuclear weapons, moreover, would lead to the proliferation and sophistication of those weapons to nearly unimaginable levels during the Cold War period, with companies like GE leading the way. Vonnegut could sense that insidious side of the corporate world, and he decided not to be a part of it.

He got out of that world through writing fiction. In

UNDERSTANDING KURT VONNEGUT

the 1950s a writer could make a living selling short stories to magazines like *Collier's* and *Redbook*. After he
began doing so, Vonnegut quit his job at GE and moved
with his family to Cape Cod, Massachusetts. Though
he would spend some of his time teaching, and even
open a Saab dealership, by the middle 50s Vonnegut
was making his way as a professional writer. Yet he had
a difficult time: toward the end of the 1950s the short
story market was beginning to dry up, and Vonnegut
faced the twin personal tragedies of his father's death
in 1957 and the deaths of his beloved sister Alice (of
cancer) and her husband (in a train wreck) within
twenty-four hours of each other in 1958. Alice and her
husband had four sons, three of whom Kurt and Jane
Vonnegut adopted—doubling their three-child family to
six. Alice's death left a permanent impression on Vonnegut of the randomness inherent in human existence.
He has said in several interviews that a writer achieves
unity in his works only by writing as if speaking to one
person—in his case to his dead sister.

Despite these difficulties Vonnegut was on the
verge of what would be the major phase of his career.
Abandoning science fiction, he turned to the subject
matter of World War II in *Mother Night*, to an anthropological analysis of religion in *Cat's Cradle*, and to a critique of social injustice in *God Bless You, Mr. Rosewater*.
In 1965 he began a two-year residency as a teacher at
the University of Iowa Writers' Workshop, where he
gave advice to such aspiring novelists as Gail Godwin

and John Irving. In 1967 Delacorte Press/Seymour Lawrence offered him a three-book contract and soon re-
printed all his books in hardcover. The first book of that
contract, *Slaughterhouse-Five*, was a milestone in
postmodern American literature, one that offered a
nonlinear mode of narration that, in Klinkowitz's
words, created "a radical reconnection of the historical
and the imaginary, the realistic and the fantastic, the
sequential and the simultaneous, the author and the
text."[5]

After his amazing productivity in the 1960s, a period of great national turmoil for all Americans over the
youth movement and the war in Vietnam, Vonnegut
not surprisingly seemed to run out of emotional capital
in the 1970s. After his children grew up and left home,
his marriage faltered, causing him a great deal of guilt.
He moved alone to New York City, became withdrawn
and depressed, suffered somewhat from writer's block.
His son Mark suffered a schizophrenic breakdown early
in the decade, but recovered to write a book about it
(*The Eden Express*) and become a physician. Much of
Vonnegut's work can be seen as his attempt to work
through familial guilt of one sort or another and to suggest ways that other lonely Americans might recover
that psychic necessity so often subverted by modern
ways of living—the extended family. *Breakfast of Champions* (1973) and *Slapstick* (1976) are essentially stories
about the disintegration of families. Fortunately,
though they did not work well as fiction—especially in

UNDERSTANDING KURT VONNEGUT

the case of *Slapstick*—these books did help Vonnegut to work through emotional problems that had plagued him since childhood.

Vonnegut's resurgence in the 1980s, heralded in 1979 by his marriage to photographer Jill Krementz and the publication of *Jailbird*, has been striking. In four strong novels and in *Palm Sunday* he has shown both a continuation of the general autobiographical direction of his fiction as well as a devotion to what might be called issues of citizenship: concern for civil liberties, the preservation of the earth's ecology, arms control. As a spokesman for such organizations as the American Civil Liberties Union and PEN, the international writers' association, he has demanded that America live up to the ideals in the Constitution and the Bill of Rights. For so long criticized as a mere Pied Piper of the young, in his mature years Vonnegut has obviously lived up to his ideal of making "a sincere effort to be a responsible elder in society."[7]

Overview

On one hand, it is easy to view Vonnegut as the simplest of writers—one who offers his readers short sentences, short paragraphs, cartoonlike characters, and lots of jokes. On the other, it is also possible to describe him in the complex terminology of postmodern criticism—as a highly experimental metafictionalist, structural anthropologist, player of intricate semiotic games. Vonnegut's writing is "metafictional" because it often calls attention to its own artificiality so as to question the conventions of traditional narrative—much as an anthropologist implicitly critiques his own culture when exploring another, or when a semiotician (literally, one who studies signs) uses language to explain how language works. Surprisingly, these contradictory images of Vonnegut as both simple and complex have coexisted with rather than undercut each other. Speaking in 1980 of Vonnegut's work in the late 1960s and early 1970s, Klinkowitz wrote that "the academic argument . . . that 'experimental' fiction had refined itself beyond the appreciation of popular readers is confounded at every turn by Vonnegut's commercial success."[8] That Vonnegut is at once simple and complex, that he has appealed to both a popular and an academic audience, in itself suggests he is a writer worthy of attention.

His simplicity stems from his background in journalism, his common sense and lack of pretension, and his desire to reach a wide audience so as to present his concerns about pressing social issues. In an interview he distanced himself from the sort of writers for whom language itself is the primary concern: "I'm not inclined to play Henry Jamesian games because they'll exclude too many people from reading the book. . . . I have made my books easy to read, punctuated carefully, with lots of white space."[9] By the time he published *Cat's*

UNDERSTANDING KURT VONNEGUT

Cradle Vonnegut had perfected his style of short sentences in short paragraphs in short chapters. Defending himself against the frequently leveled charge that his work is simplistic rather than simple, he remarks in *Palm Sunday* that "it has been my experience with literary critics and academics in this country that clarity looks a lot like laziness and ignorance and childishness and cheapness to them."[10]

Yet underneath the simple surface of his work Vonnegut is certainly complex enough. His complexity stems from two sources: his scientifically sophisticated view of the world and the innovative way he conveys that view through his fiction. Trained in chemistry and anthropology, given to quoting the likes of Stephen Jay Gould and Carl Sagan, Vonnegut brings to his fiction a different sensibility than does the average American novelist. Closer to a scientifically minded writer like Thomas Pynchon than to Henry James, Vonnegut creates *science* fiction—even when his work has nothing to do with visitors from outer space. As James Lundquist puts it, in his novels Vonnegut strives "to reveal new viewpoints in somewhat the same way the theory of relativity broke through the concepts of absolute space and time."[11]

Vonnegut's view of things is essentially that of most modern scientists: that we live in an unimaginably vast cosmos which has existed for billions of years before life evolved on this planet and which will probably exist for billions of years after life is extinguished here;

that space and time themselves are relative, so that the human point of view alone makes people see the universe as they do; and that in particular the claims of various religions concerning God or the afterlife may serve a psychological function in human culture but are based on literally no evidence whatsoever. In regard to his religious stance Vonnegut remarked that "my ancestors, who came to the United States a little before the Civil War, were atheists. So I'm not rebelling against organized religion. I never had any."[12] Philosophically, Vonnegut comes closest to existentialists like Albert Camus and Jean-Paul Sartre. As Peter J. Reed writes, in Vonnegut as in the existentialists,

no identifiable meaning or purpose to existence is presumed. The workings of the cosmos remain inscrutable. Where man comes from, why he is here, where he goes to, remain unanswerable. So man continues self-consciously alone, reluctant to accept the fact of his *being* without knowing *why*, anxious to find reason, purpose, and order in the universe and in his relationship to it, but seeing instead only that things happen, unpredictably, pointlessly and often cruelly.[13]

Quite simply, for Vonnegut the universe does not appear to have been designed as a home for human beings.

In his study *The Exploded Form*, James Mellard argues that after writers began to incorporate the new

11

UNDERSTANDING KURT VONNEGUT

understanding of Darwin into their fiction, the underlying notion for the nineteenth-century novel became *evolution*. The underlying notion of the modern novel, however, has shifted to the idea of *explosion*, as writers have turned to the big bang theory of the creation of the universe. While the nineteenth-century novel typically "fostered growth, attachment, assimilation, and integration," Mellard writes, the modern novel "presents decay, detachment, alienation, disintegration." Mellard lists John Barth, Donald Barthelme, Richard Brautigan, Robert Coover, William Gass, and Vonnegut as the principal postmodern creators of the "exploded" novel form. In his 1980 study Mellard was describing Vonnegut's metafictional novels of the 1960s and 70s; but he accurately predicted the change in Vonnegut's work in the 1980s when he suggested that the mode of fiction after writers had exhausted the literature of "explosion"—in which traditional plotting, characterization, and thematic coherence were often abandoned—would "probably be a new realism."[14] In fact, Vonnegut's career can be divided into three major phases: science fiction, metafiction, and "neorealism." All three are his attempts to reflect the anxiety of our age as our paradigms of nature change.

But there are compensations for the anxiety of being human in Vonnegut's fiction. As Giannone observes, "Out of a sense of helplessness before cosmic anarchy, Vonnegut turns to the formative power of art to restore himself."[15] As Vonnegut himself confesses,

UNDERSTANDING KURT VONNEGUT

"Most of my adult life has been spent bringing some kind of order to sheets of paper eight and a half inches wide and eleven inches long. This severely limited activity has allowed me to ignore many a storm."[16] Vonnegut's fiction includes many artist figures who strive to bring order to experience by writing, painting, composing music. If the pessimistic side of Vonnegut leads him to bemoan the chaos of madness, war, and cosmic entrophy, the other side causes him to celebrate and marvel at the persistence of the human spirit in the face of that disorder as it pursues and gives aesthetic pleasure.

Aside from artist figures Vonnegut's fiction is filled with other recurrent character types that reflect his thematic preoccupations. In all the novels one finds unenlightened "straights"—naïve believers in the sanctity of their company, their country, their religion. While Vonnegut usually shows a great deal of sympathy for such characters, he always overturns their settled view of things by introducing a character from outside their situation who offers an anthropological critique of their beliefs. In the most extreme form this character is a visitor from outer space, like the Tralfamadorians in *Slaughterhouse-Five*. At other times he is simply from another culture, or from another state of mind because of his experiences in extreme situations like madness or war. As he said in an interview, "It's a tremendous advantage to be at the edge. . . , because you can make a better commentary than someone at the center would."[17] The essence of that commentary is the under-standing that systems of human belief always refer more to themselves than to the actual state of things in the cosmos.

Vonnegut not only gives the reader recurrent char-acter types: he gives recurrent characters. By including figures from earlier novels in later ones he has created what Klinkowitz calls a "mod Yoknapatawpha County"[18] resembling Faulkner's imaginary world of re-current characters. Howard Campbell, the Nazi propa-gandist and double agent; Eliot Rosewater, the philan-thropist and science fiction fan; Celia Hoover, the Indi-ana beauty who swallows Drano—all appear and reap-pear throughout Vonnegut's work. The down-and-out science fiction writer Kilgore Trout is clearly Vonnegut's most persistent such character. Trout, whose scores of novels appear only as cheap paperbacks with lurid cov-ers, is a sort of alter ego for Vonnegut—what he feared he might become had he continued to be typecast as a sci-fi hack. Always out of money, having to find a new publisher for every novel, putting off people at every turn because of his lack of social skills, Trout neverthe-less possesses genuine insight into "what is really going on"—a constant refrain in Vonnegut's fiction. By re-counting the plots of Trout's many books, Vonnegut is able to make thematic points about the limitations of the anthropomorphic point of view.

Beginning with his 1966 preface to *Mother Night*, Vonnegut has become more and more autobiographical with each novel. In a series of prologues to his recent fiction he has been explicitly so, drawing direct parallels between his fiction and his life. In these later works a guilt-ridden protagonist looks back on his past and tries to come to terms with his ineffectual parents, who because of their own emotional problems were unable to give sufficient love to their son. The son's guilt arises out of his parents' difficulties as well as his own, which may include failed marriages, professional problems, or actual crimes like perjury or manslaughter. Because he has lost his family, either literally or emotionally, the guilty protagonist longs for or tries to create an artificial extended family—a group of fellow bureaucrats, soldiers, painters—who help each other get through their lonely lives.

Aside from the cold comfort of black humor or simply being freed from life's comforting illusions, Vonnegut's fiction offers a warmer vision of at least the possibility of a human community based not on pseudostatements about the nature of the cosmos but on simple decency and love. Like such realists and skeptics before him as Twain and Stephen Crane, Vonnegut comes to the conclusion that once one sees the universe is indifferent to man, human solidarity becomes all the more necessary. As Clark Mayo observes, in Vonnegut's work "there are no Nirvanas, yet Vonnegut does believe in the possibility of being human with some grace and dignity in a world which, as Hemingway so often wrote, will break or kill you eventually."[19]

And as Eliot Rosewater puts it even more bluntly, the first thing newborns should be told is "God damn it, babies, you've got to be kind."[20] Rosewater himself embodies Vonnegut's ideal of uncritical love, for he gives away his fortune and even adopts all the needy children of his home county. Yet Vonnegut is always aware of the dangers inherent in his advocacy of this sort of unconditional love—that it may prove illusory or hopelessly sentimental. But Robert Scholes, by way of defending him against that charge writes, "Vonnegut is a vulgar sentimentalist—a quality he shares with, Dickens, for instance."[21] Perhaps the best way to begin understanding Kurt Vonnegut is to keep in mind his epigraph to *Bluebeard*, which is a line out of a letter to him from his son Mark: "We are here to help each other get through this thing, whatever it is."

Notes

1. "Vonnegut in America," *Vonnegut in America*, ed. Jerome Klinkowitz and Donald L. Lawler (New York: Delacorte/Lawrence, 1977) 33. For further biographical information on Vonnegut see 7–36.

2. *Conversations with Kurt Vonnegut*, ed. William Rodney Allen (Jackson: University Press of Mississippi, 1988) 89. Hereafter *CKV*.

3. *CKV* 162.

4. Richard Giannone, *Vonnegut: A Preface to His Novels* (Port Washington, NY: Kennikat Press, 1977) 6.

5. Jerome Klinkowitz, *Kurt Vonnegut* (New York: Methuen, 1982) 69.

6. *Palm Sunday* (New York: Delacorte/Lawrence, 1981) 189.

7. *CKV* 273.

8. "Postface: 1980," *Literary Disruptions*, 2nd ed. (Urbana: University of Illinois Press, 1980) 197.

9. *CKV* 48.

10. *Palm Sunday* 320.

11. James Lundquist, *Kurt Vonnegut* (New York: Ungar, 1976) 71.

12. *CKV* 78.

13. Peter J. Reed, *Kurt Vonnegut, Jr.* (New York: Warner, 1972) 206.

14. James Mellard, *The Exploded Form* (Urbana: University of Illinois Press, 1980) 11, 16, 22.

15. Giannone 122–23.

16. *Palm Sunday* 321.

17. *CKV* 299.

18. "Kurt Vonnegut, Jr. and the Crime of His Times," *The Vonnegut Statement*, ed. Jerome Klinkowitz and John Somer (New York: Delacorte/Lawrence, 1973) 38.

19. Clark Mayo, *Kurt Vonnegut: The Gospel from Outer Space* (San Bernardino: R. Reginald/Borgo Press, 1977) 5.

20. *God Bless You, Mr. Rosewater* (New York: Delacorte/Lawrence, 1971) 93.

21. Robert Scholes, "Chasing a Lone Eagle: Vonnegut's College Writing," in *Vonnegut Statement* 45.

CHAPTER TWO

Player Piano; The Sirens of Titan

Although the 1950s have been called the age of conformity, some Americans had trouble fitting into their peacetime roles in the new consumer society. Like many young men just back from the war who entered the business world for the first time—a world promising an ever-increasing standard of living through such company mottos as "Better living through chemistry" and "Progress is our most important product"—Vonnegut soon had ambivalent feelings about his identity as a corporate soldier. Those feelings would grow until 1951, when he quit his secure job at General Electric to become a full-time writer. Not surprisingly, Vonnegut's first two novels constitute his uneasy response to the radical advances in technology that were transforming American culture in the 1950s.

In his four years as a public relations man for GE, Vonnegut saw firsthand how the enormous momentum of scientific progress built up during the crisis of the war carried over into peacetime, where if anything it accelerated to meet the pent-up desires of consumers for

17

washing machines, automobiles, televisions. With his background in science Vonnegut was fascinated by the technological wonders he saw at GE—fascinated but also disturbed. As he recalls in an interview, after seeing an automated milling machine developed by one of the company's engineers, he was startled to find that "this damned machine was able to do as good a job as most of the machinists ever could." It did not take him long to conclude that "industry was dedicated to devising ways to run its machines without people."[1] Quite simply, this perception of the human cost of technological "progress" was the seed of Vonnegut's career as a novelist.

That Vonnegut began by writing science fiction was, given his background, almost inevitable. As he put it, "There was no avoiding it, since the General Electric Company *was* science fiction."[2] General Electric "was" science fiction in the sense that it quickly turned the imaginable into the real—pure science into applied technology. As a genre sci-fi does much the same thing, except that what it imagines is at the time so technologically advanced that it can be made "real" only on paper. Thus one of the attractions of sci-fi is its almost self-contradictory character: based on science, the essence of which is adherence to fact, it is nevertheless fiction, which can ignore fact in the free play of the imagination. Science fiction can extend from futuristic realism to pure fantasy, a range Vonnegut himself displays in the gritty

PLAYER PIANO

familiarity of *Player Piano* versus the cosmic zaniness of *The Sirens of Titan*.[3]

At its best, science fiction has something for the technocrat as well as the artist, the satirist of contemporary culture as well as the cultural prophet, the utopian optimist as well as the Orwellian doomsayer. In *God Bless You, Mr. Rosewater*, Vonnegut has his protagonist praise a convention of sci-fi writers: "I love you sons of bitches. You're all I read any more. You're the only ones who'll talk about the really important changes going on."[4] Carl Sagan's novel *Contact* is a recent example of science fiction offering this sort of intellectual scope. At its worst, though, sci-fi can be cheap hack work devoid of meaningful characterization or any sense of style. Not surprisingly, Vonnegut's mixed feelings about scientific "progress" parallel his reservations about being labeled a science fiction writer after publishing *Player Piano* and *The Sirens of Titan*. While admitting the influence of such respected literary models as *Brave New World* and *1984*, he has been careful to distance himself from a genre he often finds self-indulgent and softheaded. As he explained in an interview, "I resent a lot of science fiction. This promising of great secrets which are just beyond our grasp—I don't think they exist. . . . The mysteries that remain to be solved have to do with relating to each other."[5]

Player Piano

In *Player Piano* Vonnegut's emphasis is clearly on the effects of technology on his characters' emotions and on those characters' relationships with each other rather than on the technology itself. The novel is set in the future, ten years after that staple of science fiction, the Third World War; yet the world Vonnegut describes is an extension of 1952 rather than a radical break from it. As Jerome Klinkowitz remarks, Vonnegut "makes his own failed paradise simpler and more familiar than the anti-utopian models of Aldous Huxley's *Brave New World* or George Orwell's *1984*. His Americans are neither drugged nor thought-controlled; they're simply bored. . . . People act the same, think the same, and have neither more nor less trouble with political repression than they had before."[6] Thus *Player Piano* is near the "realistic" pole of science fiction; its aim is more to satirize corporate life in the 1950s than to fantasize about a profoundly different world in the distant future.

Vonnegut's protagonist, Paul Proteus, at first seems like a confident, unquestioning, 1950s-style junior executive on his way up the corporate ladder. At age thirty-five he already manages the vast Illium works, a complex of machines turning out "parts for baby carriages and bottle caps, motorcycles and refrigerators, televisions sets and tricycles—the fruits of peace."[7] "The most important, brilliant person in Illium" (1), he seems perfectly in command in the opening scene as he corrects a problem with a malfunctioning lathe in Building 58. But as Vonnegut will make clear in the course of the novel, Proteus himself is potentially a sort of Building 58—an anachronistic glitch in the rigidly engineered machine of the corporate state.

The corporate world of *Player Piano* is a simple, efficient one with just three parts: the machines themselves and, divided in Illium by the Iroquois River, the managerial/engineering elite versus the idle masses provided for by the government. As a product of his class Paul at first reassures himself that "things really were better than ever. For once after the great bloodbath of the war, the world really was cleared of unnatural terrors—mass starvation, mass imprisonment, mass torture, mass murder" (6). Yet in more introspective moods he admits the undemocratic nature of the new order: "This elite business, this assurance of superiority, this sense of rightness about the hierarchy topped by managers and engineers—this was instilled in all college graduates, and there were no bones about it" (5). Paul's lingering sense of guilt about his privileged position sets him apart from nearly all his colleagues and aligns him with such literary archetypes as the Prince in Twain's *The Prince and the Pauper* and such religious figures as the Buddha. In each case a privileged person gives up his position and discovers profound moral truths by identifying with the poor.

Yet the "poor" in *Player Piano* ironically have everything—everything but a sense of self-worth. As Paul explains in a speech to his peers that may nail down a big promotion for him, the masses have been affected by two industrial revolutions. The first was the conventional Industrial Revolution—the creation of powered machines in the 1800s, which displaced many manual laborers. The second occurred when computers took over routine mental work in the second half of the twentieth century, displacing millions of lower-level white-collar workers. In *Player Piano* these displaced ones keep to their side of the river, where they idle in bars or kill time with make-work assignments in the Reconstruction and Reclamation Corps. The "Reeks and Wrecks," as they cynically call themselves, may desultorily fill a few potholes and sweep the streets, but usually just lean on their shovels and complain about "the system." In Marxian terms they are the proletariat of the future: no longer enslaved by the privileged class, they have been rendered useless by its machines, but are alienated and ripe for revolution should the right leader emerge to focus their anger.

Even more threatening than the masses to the corporate state, however, is what Paul calls the Third Revolution in Industry—the taking over of abstract thought by computers with artificial intelligence. Proteus realizes that soon the managers and engineers will put themselves out of work by integrating all of American industry "into one stupendous Rube Goldberg machine" (4). His friend Bud Calhoun, who possesses the peculiarly American "restless, erratic insight and imagi-

PLAYER PIANO

nation of a gadgeteer" (4), has automated his industrial division only to find that the system he improved now has no place for him. Those managers who still have jobs are struggling up a corporate ladder rapidly growing narrower and narrower, dropping rung after rung as automation proceeds at a geometric rate.

Throughout *Player Piano* Vonnegut effectively satirizes the frantic quality of corporate careerism in the 1950s. His portrait of the back-stabbing "company man," in the person of Dr. Lawson Shepherd, Paul's assistant, is sharply drawn. Resentful in his position as Paul's subordinate, Shepherd hopes to get ahead by informing on his boss whenever he comes in late for work or keeps company with "undesirables." For Shepherd, "life seemed to be laid out like a golf course, with a series of beginnings, hazards, and ends, and with a definite summing up—for comparisons with each other's scores—after each hole" (43). Though he fails to triumph in the corporate game with Paul, by the end of the novel Shepherd has "won" Paul's wife.

Anita Proteus is one of the most unpleasant characters in Vonnegut's early fiction. She is drawn to Shepherd as *Player Piano* progresses because she is his female counterpart—the competitive corporate wife of the 1950s. In her opening conversation with Paul she reveals herself as scheming, manipulative, other-directed to an extreme. Her only thought is that he should butter up his powerful bosses, Kroner and Baer, so that they will reward him with the promotion in Pittsburgh. "Getting Pittsburgh" becomes Anita's obsessive concern as she tries to suppress Paul's doubts about the system and keep him on the straight and narrow way up. Whenever the two quarrel, they end their conversations with a mechanical "I love you, Paul . . . And I love *you*, Anita," phrases that grow more hollow with each repetition. Even early on, Paul's interior musings suggest that their life together has little chance of working out: "Anita had the mechanics of marriage down pat, even to the subtlest conventions. If her approach was disturbingly rational, systematic, she was thorough enough to turn out a creditable counterfeit of warmth" (16). If Paul is a Building 58 in the corporate machine—one that doesn't work well because of its age and idiosyncrasies—Anita is a state-of-the-art component, "turning out" her product with ruthless efficiency. But what she manufactures—home life—is only a counterfeit of the real thing. Thus Paul is frustrated in both the public and private spheres, since his wife is determined to make the two merely identical.

From a contemporary perspective Anita is as much victim as villain—a victim of the restrictive sexual roles possible to women in the 1950s. Denied any meaningful work of her own, she is left to get vicarious pleasure out of her husband's accomplishments. Vonnegut chose to keep Paul and Anita childless so as to make their breakup simpler in moral terms and more believable to the audience of the times; but Anita's childlessness leaves her without the maternal concerns of most

PLAYER PIANO

women. Lacking a career or children, she is empty, and is left with only the pursuit of status to fill the void.

For Anita the ultimate triumph would be for Paul to be promoted by Kroner and Baer—the "chief executive officers," in contemporary business terminology, of "the entire Eastern Division." But Paul sees flaws in his bosses that reflect those of the system at large. Baer "was a social cretin," yet he "embodied the knowledge and technique of industry"; while Kroner, who had "a poor record as an engineer," nevertheless "personified the faith, the near-holiness, the spirit of the complicated venture, . . . the priceless quality of believing in the system, and of making others believe in it too, and do as they were told." Paul concludes that "together, they made an approximately whole man" (38).

Kroner soon becomes the dominant force for Paul in the novel. Complicating their relationship is the fact that Kroner had been Paul's father's closest friend—and that George Proteus had been a brilliant engineer and absolute believer in the system. Vonnegut is obviously self-consciously setting up a Freudian oedipal relationship between Paul and Kroner, the representative of his dead father. When the two meet, "Kroner's enormous, hairy hand closed about Paul's and Paul, inspite [sic] of himself, felt docile, and loving, and childlike. It was as though Paul stood in the enervating, emasculating presence of his father again" (37). Like Anita, Kroner will try to "emasculate" Paul by having him deny his true identity as a rebel against the corporate state. As Paul expresses it, in thoughts suggesting the strongly sexual aspects of the system, he lacks "what so many had: the sense of spiritual importance in what they were doing; the ability to be moved emotionally, almost like a lover, by the great omnipresent and omniscient spook of the corporate persona" (55). Thus *Player Piano* is in part, like *Brave New World* and *1984*, a battle for the protagonist's erotic identity, a struggle of the individual to love what he—not the state—wills.

If Kroner is Paul's "bad father," the evil role model urging him, paradoxically, to behave himself and quietly fit into the system, then Ed Finnerty is the "good father" urging Paul to rebel. Having come to Illium with Paul years earlier, Finnerty had been promoted to Washington and so had been away. But he shows up the day of Paul's big speech and announces he has quit his top-level position. Thinking back on Finnerty's casual habits of dress, his hard drinking and womanizing, Paul realizes that "Finnerty's way of life wasn't as irrational as it seemed: that it was, in fact, a studied and elaborate insult to the managers and engineers of Illium, and to their immaculate wives" (30). It is of course inevitable that Finnerty and Anita will quarrel, and they do—viciously. But Paul is drawn to his brilliant but out-of-work friend; and he "wondered about his own deep drives as he realized how much pleasure he was getting from recollections of Finnerty's socially destructive, undisciplined antics" (31). The term "deep drives" has the unmistakable ring of cocktail-party talk based on a casual knowledge of Freud's theories one could hear throughout the 1950s. Finnerty becomes a sort of lay psychiatrist for Paul, helping him discover within himself "a rebellious streak that Paul was only beginning to suspect" (31).

Paul's transformation from frustrated but loyal corporate soldier to revolutionary is the dramatic center of *Player Piano*, so Vonnegut is careful to maintain suspense for most of the novel by having his protagonist vacillate between his attractions to Kroner and Finnerty. After Finnerty shows up drunk at the dinner party featuring Paul's speech, Paul thinks that "the brilliant liberal, the iconoclast, the freethinker he had admired in his youth now proved to be no more than sick, repellent" (41). Yet after Finnerty bets on Paul to beat a computerized checker-playing machine rigged up by some junior engineers as postdinner entertainment, and Paul wins this futuristic update of the nineteenth-century folk tale of John Henry versus the steam engine, Paul goes out for drinks with Finnerty on the other side of the river. There his "conversion" begins.

At the run-down neighborhood bar, which is such a stark contrast to the elegant dining room they have just left, Finnerty opens up and explains why he quit his job: "I want to stay as close to the edge as I can without going over. Out on the edge you see all kinds of things you can't see from the center" (73). As part of his desire to get Paul "off center," Finnerty introduces him to James Lasher, a chaplain in the Reconstruction and Reclamation Corps who serves as a mouthpiece for Vonnegut to advance ideas he encountered in his year of graduate study in anthropology at the University of Chicago. Lasher explains the discontentment of the masses quite simply: "You people have engineered them out of their part in the economy.... What's left is just about zero.... Their whole culture's been shot to hell" (78). Noting that traditional religious faith is waning, Lasher believes things "are ripe for a phony Messiah, and when he comes, it's sure to be a bloody business" (80).

Impressed by Lasher's theoretical explanations of the malaise of society, and getting drunk as he listens, Paul decides that "this was *real*, this side of the river, and [he] loved these common people, and wanted to help, and let them know they were loved and understood, and he wanted them to love him too" (88). But Vonnegut does not present Paul's drunken feeling of "generalized love" without irony: like many privileged liberal intellectuals having their fling with the masses, Paul is still slumming, still inwardly holding on to part of his sense of superiority to the Homesteaders, still preserving a sense of his individuality. This initial attempt of Finnerty to "recruit" Paul ends with Finnerty "savagely improvising" on the bar's player piano—the source of the novel's title, and an obvious symbol for the individual's stubborn need to perform his own unique song rather than listen to the mechanical score of the machine.

PLAYER PIANO

If Lasher is Vonnegut's mouthpiece in the guise of the academically trained anthropologist, the Shah of Bratpuhr is a comic lay version of the same thing. As "spiritual leader of 6,000,000 members of the Kolhouri sect" (16) the Shah offers ironic comment on the fruits of "developed" society as he tours the United States for the first time. Although his guide insists the Reeks and Wrecks are affluent, happy citizens, the Shah more truthfully refers to them as "slaves." As Clark Mayo points out, the Shah's purpose is to ask "questions which are ubiquitous in Vonnegut's fiction: why? ("why hurry?") and what? ("what are people for?")."[8] When he asks the latter question of EPICAC, the supercomputer proudly shown off by his State Department guide, the Shah gets no answer. Speaking for Vonnegut, he calls EPICAC a "false god" (106). Like Lasher the Shah has a weakness for the bottle (his sipping of Sumklish, the "sacred Kolhouri drink," becomes a recurrent joke in his periodic appearances in the novel) that excuses his uninhibited assessments of America's flaws. In a novel whose dominant modes are at times bitter satire and even flirtations with tragedy, the Shah provides comic relief. As is the case with the fool in *King Lear*, his comic mask allows him to get away with speaking truths that from another mouth might infuriate the hearer. Mayo notes that the Shah is in effect the first of a recurrent character type in Vonnegut's fiction—the visitor from another planet, whose perceptions "enable us to see more clearly beneath the surface of our own society."[9] Vonnegut drives home the point by having the Shah end up by accident on the revolutionary side at the novel's end.

While the Shah's comic subplot connects only casually with the main line of action, the ideal of a preindustrial culture that Bratpuhr represents also appears in Paul's world—in two opposite forms. Paul decides to try the Thoreauvian experiment of living the "natural" life when he buys a farm. His aim is to take Anita away from her leisure-ridden life and give her the blessing of household chores. But Anita will have none of it, preferring instead to cannibalize the farmhouse for decorative knickknacks for their house back in town. Paul is forced to conclude that "the charming little cottage he'd taken as a symbol of the good life of a farmer was as irrelevant as a statue of Venus at the gate of a sewage-disposal plant" (224). The second "pastoral" possibility is the corporate version—an island called the Meadows where the top managers go to a sort of Boy Scout camp for adults. Having been made the captain of one of the four teams in competition with each other, Paul is expected to show the proper spirit by singing inane fight songs at the top of his lungs and taunting his opponents with practical jokes. The Meadows' games include "capture the flag, Indian wrestling, touch football, shuffleboard, and trying to throw the other captains in the lake" (119). This corporate parody of getting back to nature disgusts Paul, and he becomes convinced that he should follow Finnerty's example and quit his job.

PLAYER PIANO

From a contemporary perspective it is easy to understand the source of the paranoic atmosphere of the novel—a book whose unstated but central question is "Whose side are you on?" That source is unquestionably the obsessive anticommunist mentality that began to build up in America immediately after World War II and climaxed in the attempts of Senator Joseph McCarthy and his followers to ferret out communists who had supposedly infiltrated every level of American government. The constitutional rights of citizens were thrown out the window at McCarthy's Committee on Un-American Activities hearings, at which witnesses were expected to inform on their left-wing friends in order to demonstrate that they themselves were not communists. *Player Piano* is implicitly Vonnegut's warning against the recurrent American problem of witch-hunting, since its hero is exactly the sort of potential subversive who would have been pursued relentlessly by McCarthyites.

The 1950s fears of an internal communist takeover of the United States proved delusional; in the futuristic setting of *Player Piano*, however, the threat of revolution turns out to be real. As Paul learns from Kroner, and eventually from Kroner's boss, the National Industrial, Commercial, Communications, Foodstuffs, and Resources Director, Dr. Frances Gelhorne, the opposition has created a loose but national organization called the Ghost Shirt Society dedicated to smashing the machines and instituting a new social order. At a tense meeting

UNDERSTANDING KURT VONNEGUT

Gelhorne reveals his plan to have Paul become a double agent by pretending to fire him and then having Paul use his contacts with Finnerty and Lasher to infiltrate the Ghost Shirts. The double agent will become a recurrent character in Vonnegut's fiction, most notably in *Mother Night*; like the anthropologist or the visitor from space, the double agent can perceive things about the workings of society that are invisible to the average person. Since he must "be" two contradictory identities at once, he sees all issues from both sides: the result is either extraordinary perceptivity or madness. Although Paul responds to Gelhorne's double agent plan by shouting "I quit," Gelhorne takes that to mean Paul is simply going along with the pretense that he has been fired.

That Vonnegut is satirizing anticommunism is apparent at several points in the last third of the novel. Lasher refers to those in the movement as "fellow travelers" (258), a phrase for communists widely recognized in the 1950s. Having been "fired," Paul feels the effects of being "blacklisted" in the way many suspected communists did in McCarthy's time, when they suddenly could not find work. When Paul returns to Illium and begins to frequent the Homestead Bar, where he met Lasher, he is drugged by Finnerty and Lasher with "truth serum," an obsessive concern of anticommunists in the 1950s who feared brainwashing techniques involving drugging the victim, then submitting him to communist indoctrination. But although Lasher and

PLAYER PIANO

Finnerty drug Paul and grill him just like the evil communists of McCarthyite fantasy, Paul's sympathies, and
Vonnegut's, are clearly with them.

Player Piano is thus an inversion of the values of
McCarthyism: the boosters of the corporate American
way are the villains while the subversives are the heroes. Vonnegut underscores his sympathies for the
leaders of the Ghost Shirts by making them intellectual
pragmatists rather than fanatical "true believers." In explaining the name for their revolutionary "army,"
Lasher recounts the story of the plains Indians who convinced themselves in the late 1800s that they could defeat the apparently triumphant white man by wearing
shirts with the magical power to stop the white soldiers'
bullets. While this absurd idea didn't win any battles,
it at least rallied the Indians for a heroic last stand.
Player Piano's Ghost Shirts actually have a uniform consisting of "a white shirt fringed in an imitation of a
buckskin shirt, and decorated with thunderbirds and
stylized buffalo worked into the fabric with brightly in-
sulated bits of wire" (250). As Lasher admits to Paul,
"We don't deny it's childish. At the same time, we admit that we've got to be a little childish, anyway, to get
the big following we need" (251). Thus *Player Piano*
demonstrates Vonnegut's skepticism about all mass
movements, whether they originate from the right or
the left. As an agnostic Vonnegut doubts the truth of
the quasi-religious underpinnings of most political en-
thusiasms; yet he knows that human beings desperately

need to believe in something larger than themselves—need to belong to a community, even if that community is based on a myth.

Yet the Ghost Shirts prove to be just as out of touch with reality as were their Indian namesakes. The dream of smashing the corporate state begins to fade when Kroner's men recapture Paul from Lasher. Placed on trial in a McCarthyesque atmosphere, he confesses he is the leader of the Ghost Shirts. The prosecuting attorney then tears down his belief that he has gone over to the other side for idealistic reasons by offering a convincing argument that Paul simply has an unresolved Oedipus complex—that his anger at the state is simply transferred anger at his dead father. Crushed, Paul admits to himself that "a moment before, he had been a glib mouthpiece for a powerful, clever organization. Now, suddenly, he was all alone, dealing with a problem singularly his own" (274).

As Paul's supposed ideals crumble into private neuroses, the heroic Ghost Shirts devolve into a drunken, indiscriminately violent mob at the novel's end, burning museums along with the factories. In a few cities the riots temporarily succeed in throwing the government forces on the defensive, but everywhere else the revolt fails miserably. As Klinkowitz observes, the plot of *Player Piano* "takes the form of a large circle," with postrevolt conditions "ending up almost precisely where they began."[10] Like most satires the novel concludes with the world in pretty much the same old mess: the Reeks and Wrecks begin repairing the machines they had smashed, and Paul, Finnerty, and Lasher resignedly head for a government roadblock to turn themselves in. So Paul Proteus, named for the Greek god of the sea who could change his shape at will, undergoes a final transformation as he abandons his identity as a revolutionary—and is engulfed once more by the corporate state.

The Sirens of Titan

After *Player Piano* Vonnegut did not publish another novel for seven years. In the interval he wrote short stories for such magazines as *Collier's* and the *Saturday Evening Post*, stories later collected in *Canary in a Cat House*.[11] With an eye on the marketplace Vonnegut became highly conscious of his middle-class audience—and learned to write accordingly. As he said in an interview, during these years "I was a very earnest student writer and had a teacher, Kenneth Littauer, an old-time magazine and editor. . . . I learned from Littauer about pace and point of view, things that are discussed in *Writer's Digest*, decent and honorable things to know."[12]

Not surprisingly, the *Sirens of Titan* showed the ill effects of Vonnegut's long layoff from novel writing since *Player Piano*. While *Player Piano* is a tightly focused satire of corporate life, *The Sirens of Titan* finally lacks a coherent center. Vonnegut betrayed the book's casual beginnings in an interview in which he recalled how an editor had asked him at a party why he hadn't written another novel. Vonnegut had improvised: "I had no idea at all for a book . . . but I started talking and told him the story of *The Sirens of Titan*."[13] Diffused thematically, inconsistent in terms of characterization and tone, Vonnegut's second novel wanders from subject to subject, from attacks on America's class system to lampoons of the military to parodies of fundamentalist preachers.[14] If in *Player Piano* Vonnegut was too controlled, in *The Sirens of Titan* he loosened up too much—even though this shaking off of constraints would have positive results for his later fiction.

The plot of the book suggests how far Vonnegut had traveled in the direction of pure fantasy from the relative realism of his first novel. Set in the distant future *The Sirens of Titan* centers on two characters: Malachi Constant and Niles Rumfoord. While traveling in a spaceship, before the novel's action opens, Rumfoord had accidentally entered a "chrono-synclastic infindibulum"[15]—a sort of time warp that causes him to materialize and dematerialize all over the solar system. In the opening scene Malachi Constant, the richest man in America, slips through a gawking crowd into Rumfoord's estate in Newport, Rhode Island, with the aim of viewing one of Rumfoord's rematerializations. Rumfoord had invited Malachi in order to reveal to him a bizzare prophecy: Constant will go to Mars with Rumfoord's wife, Beatrice, impregnate her on the way, and

THE SIRENS OF TITAN

have a son named Chrono by her. Having been in the chrono-synclastic infindibulum, Rumfoord knows the future because he has already experienced it; as he tells Malachi, "Everything that ever has been will always be, and everything that ever will be always has been" (26). Here is the first appearance of the nonlinear conception of time that will pervade Vonnegut's subsequent fiction and be so thematically important in *Slaughterhouse-Five*.

Malachi and Beatrice do all they can to avoid Rumfoord's prophecy, but nothing works. Malachi tries dissipation, throwing a wild party in Hollywood lasting nearly two months, while Beatrice berates her husband whenever he materializes for not treating her with respect and telling her how to avoid all the unsettling events he sees in her future. But as Rumfoord explains, the future simply *is*, and cannot be altered. In a striking image he compares life to a roller coaster ride: "I can see the whole roller coaster you're on. And sure—I could . . . tell you about every dip and turn, warn you about every bogeyman that was going to pop out at you in the tunnels. But that wouldn't help you any. . . . Because you'd *still* have to take the roller coaster ride" (57–58).

The rest of *The Sirens of Titan* is a cosmic roller coaster ride from Earth to Mars, from Mars to Mercury, from Mercury back to Earth, and finally to one of Saturn's moons, Titan. Malachi and Beatrice are kidnapped by Martians, who plan an invasion of Earth. They brainwash Malachi, give him the name Unk, and put him in the Martian army. There, under the orders of his superiors, he strangles his best friend, Stoney Stevenson, a rebellious Martian commander who parallels Ed Finnerty in *Player Piano*. Rumfoord turns out to be masterminding the whole invasion, one he alone knows will fail. His actual aim is to set up a new religion, the Church of God of the Utterly Indifferent, based on a fanciful interpretation of the meaning of the failed invasion. Rumfoord saves Unk/Malachi from death in the invasion by detouring him and another soldier, Boaz, to Mercury for three years. He then brings him to Earth to act as a manipulated messiah (as Proteus did for the Ghost Shirts) called the Space Wanderer for Rumfoord's new religion. Finally, Rumfoord reveals to a huge crowd that Unk is Malachi Constant and that he had strangled Stoney. All this is to reinforce Rumfoord's central "religious" insight: that we are all the products of chance, of sheer accident. Rumfoord reunites a reluctant Beatrice and Chrono with Malachi, then sends them to Titan, where they learn that the history of Earth has been determined largely by beings on Tralfamadore, who simply want to help one of their space travelers repair his ship. This traveler, Salo, although a machine, learns to love Malachi on Titan, and philosophizes with him about life's meaning at the novel's end. Beatrice and Malachi finally reconcile before Malachi's death, which Salo makes pleasant by implanting the posthypnotic illusion that Malachi is being reunited with Stoney in paradise.

While Clark Mayo's suggestion that this bizarre

plot is a satire of science fiction tropes seems reasonable, his claim that "Vonnegut's second novel [is] clearly one of his best" does not.[16] Whole sections of the book, such as the episode on Mercury involving Unk's and Boaz's encounters with sound-absorbing creatures called harmoniums, seem gratuitous exercises in fantasy rather than thematically integrated elements of a larger design. Malachi's characterization is anything but constant, even given the fact that he has had his memory destroyed several times by the Martians. He is not convincing as the dissipated richest man in the world, as a zombielike private in the Martian army, or as the loving family man of the novel's end. Finally, the book's difficulties arise out of Vonnegut's inability to decide whether Malachi or Rumfoord is his central character.

While Malachi Constant never comes to life as a character, Rumfoord comes much closer to doing so. He does in part because he has a real-life model: Franklin Delano Roosevelt. "Roosevelt," Vonnegut has said, "is the key figure in the book."[17] Vonnegut's physical portrait of Rumfoord obviously suggests Roosevelt, often caricatured as the picture of optimism with a jaunty cigarette in a holder: "He put a cigarette in a long, bone cigarette holder, lighted it. He thrust out his jaw. The cigarette holder pointed straight up" (284). Alluding to Roosevelt's fatal illness during his last term, Vonnegut writes that "Rumfoord did not look well. His color was bad. And, although he smiled as always, his teeth seemed to be gnashing behind the smile" (244–45).

UNDERSTANDING KURT VONNEGUT

Like most Americans Vonnegut had ambivalent feelings about the president who spent the longest time in office and who so profoundly altered the nature of American government. Praised for getting the country out of the Depression, Roosevelt was also resented for his willingness to manipulate the public in order to put in place the sweeping social welfare programs of the New Deal. Similarly, Rumfoord appears as both a charismatic intellectual with the good of Americans at heart and a ruthless manipulator willing to brainwash his fellow Earthlings, sacrifice countless Martians in a doomed invasion, and to do so even though he realizes he is himself being manipulated by the Tralfamadorians. A striking, complex character in a weak novel, Rumfoord is important as a precursor to the sort of larger-than-life "historical" figures Vonnegut would write about in *God Bless You, Mr. Rosewater* and *Jailbird*.

In fact *The Sirens of Titan* as a whole is more important for the seeds of later techniques and thematic concerns of its author than it is in itself. Its satire of religious fundamentalism looks forward to the radical cultural relativism of *Cat's Cradle*. While such preachers as the Reverend Bobby Denton make the old mistake of interpreting every event as God's will, Rumfoord's Church of the Utterly Indifferent teaches that "luck is not the hand of God" (180). By revealing that such monuments on Earth as Stonehenge and the Great Wall of China were actually built on the telepathic orders of the Tralfamadorians to serve as messages to Salo, Rumfoord suggests the titanic effect of chance in the universe. Presumably had Salo's spaceship not broken down on Titan, Stonehenge and the Great Wall would not have been built. While humans "behaved at all times as though there were a big eye in the sky" (276), *The Sirens of Titan* suggests that that eye is often closed, looking somewhere else, or nonexistent. As the intellectual hero of the novel Rumfoord sees through all the fake programs limiting the understanding of others and breaks through to pure existential freedom. Yet Rumfoord dies alone, leaving his Eleanor Roosevelt–like wife to Malachi Constant, who adopts the less forboding philosophy that the "purpose of human life, no matter who is controlling it, is to love whoever is around to be loved" (313).

Finally *The Sirens of Titan* was a worthwhile failure in terms of its use of new techniques—techniques readers would soon begin to recognize as the distinctive Vonnegut style. Short paragraphs, often consisting of only a sentence or two, make up much of the book. In contrast to the subdued humor of *Player Piano*, *The Sirens of Titan* is filled with jokes. Whole sections of the book, in fact, are structured to lead to a punch line—with the whole novel being the joke that the great monuments of human culture actually spell out Tralfamadorian messages like "Replacement part on the way."[18] Much of the humor involves the first appearance in Vonnegut's novels of metafictional techniques—

of prefacing his chapters with epigraphs from imaginary books, of satirizing book reviewers by quoting imaginary reviews of those imaginary books, of placing the whole novel inside an editorial framework of the distant future (which suggests the Einsteinian paradox that any point in time is past, present, and future at once, depending on the point of view imposed by one's temporal "location"), and, most outrageously, of insisting that "all persons, places, and events in this book are real" (6). If nothing else, *The Sirens of Titan* shows that Vonnegut was beginning to find his distinctive voice.

Notes

1. *Conversations with Kurt Vonnegut*, ed. William Rodney Allen (Jackson: University Press of Mississippi, 1988) 199. Hereafter *CKV*.

2. *CKV* 93.

3. For a fuller treatment of Vonnegut as sci-fi writer see Karen Woods and Charles Woods, "The Vonnegut Effect: Science Fiction and Beyond," *The Vonnegut Statement*, ed. Jerome Klinkowitz and John Somer (New York: Delacorte/Lawrence, 1973) 133–57.

4. *God Bless You, Mr. Rosewater* (New York: Delacorte/Lawrence, 1971) 27.

5. *CKV* 74.

6. Jerome Klinkowitz, *Kurt Vonnegut* (New York: Methuen, 1982) 35–36.

7. *Player Piano* (New York: Delacorte/Lawrence, 1971) 3. Subsequent references are noted parenthetically.

8. Clark Mayo, *Kurt Vonnegut: The Gospel from Outer Space* (San Bernardino: R. Reginald/Borgo Press, 1977) 13.

THE SIRENS OF TITAN

10. Mayo 13.

11. Klinkowitz 36.

11. For an account of this period see Jerome Klinkowitz, "A Do-It-Yourself Story Collection by Kurt Vonnegut," *Vonnegut in America*, ed. Klinkowitz and Donald L. Lawler (New York: Delacorte/Lawrence, 1977) 51–60.

12. *CKV* 158.

13. *CKV* 35.

14. Some critics have a higher regard for *The Sirens of Titan*. See, e.g., James Mellard, "The Modes of Fiction: Or, *Player Piano* Ousts *Mechanical Bride* and *The Sirens of Titan* invade *The Guttenberg Galaxy*," *Vonnegut Statement* 178–203.

15. *The Sirens of Titan* (New York: Delacorte/Lawrence, 1971) 14. Subsequent references are noted parenthetically.

16. Mayo 15.

17. *CKV* 159.

18. Donald L. Lawler, in *"The Sirens of Titan:* Vonnegut's Metaphysical Shaggy-Dog Story," *Vonnegut in America* 61–86, sees the whole novel as the proverbial shaggy-dog joke—one which is strung out to an anticlimactic punch line.

CHAPTER THREE

Mother Night; Cat's Cradle; God Bless You, Mr. Rosewater

*P*layer *Piano*, *The Sirens of Titan*, and Vonnegut's short stories of the 1950s could be called his apprentice work; his novels of the 1960s constitute his major phase, his maturation into a writer with a unique voice. One should avoid the temptation to divide an author's career into neat phases corresponding to decades, but in Vonnegut's case such a division seems just. His fiction in the 1960s—*Mother Night; Cat's Cradle; God Bless You, Mr. Rosewater;* and *Slaughterhouse-Five*—was a qualitative improvement over that of the 1950s, just as his work in the 1970s would constitute a marked falling off from that level of achievement before his literary comeback in the 1980s.

Mother Night

Mother Night (1962) was Vonnegut's first important novel, despite the fact that it originally appeared only in paperback and was not reviewed until its reissue in 1966. The contrast between the unfocused, even sprawl-

ing quality of *The Sirens of Titan* and the tautness of
Mother Night is striking. One reason for the change was
Vonnegut's rediscovery of an old truism of fiction writing: using the first-person point of view can help provide structure and direction in a narrative. Throughout
the rest of his career, with the exception of *Slaughterhouse-Five*, Vonnegut has been at his fictional best
when allowing a distinctive, often guilt-ridden character
to tell his own story. His first such first-person narrator,
Howard W. Campbell, Jr., is a fascinating man with an
absorbing confession to make about how he has come
to the eve of his trial by the State of Israel as a Nazi war
criminal.

Like his creator Campbell is an American with German affinities—an uneasy position in which to be after,
say, 1938, one which Vonnegut would explore several
times in his fiction and often discuss in interviews.
Brought to Germany in 1923 by his parents because of
his father's work for GE, Campbell, from age eleven on,
found "my education, my friends, and my principal language were German."[1] During the 1930s he found his
vocation as a playwright in German and took a German
actress as his wife. His parents returned to America in
1939, but he stayed on, believing that a literary artist
could live outside the world of politics. The whole novel
suggests just how naïve that assumption was. Recruited
as a double agent just before the war by Frank Wirta-
nen, an agent of the United States War Department,
Campbell accepts because "as a spy of the sort he de-

scribed, I would have an opportunity for some pretty grand acting" (31). He is soon the chief "writer and broadcaster of Nazi propaganda to the English-speaking world" (21), even while the War Department is using him to send valuable information encoded in everything he says.

In his first two novels Vonnegut worked in the popular genre of science fiction; in *Mother Night* he turned to another popular form—the spy novel. As Jerome Klinkowitz points out, the conventions of the genre include "double identities, mixed loyalties, complex intrigues, suspenseful danger and hairbreadth escapes."[2] *Mother Night* provides all of that, but it goes far beyond the usual concerns of the spy thriller by exploring the metaphysical implications of the network of conscious and unconscious fictions that make up human experience. As Vonnegut announces in the introduction to the novel, which he wrote for the 1966 edition, "We are what we pretend to be, so we must be careful about what we pretend to be." (v). The issue for Campbell becomes whether he is the vicious, anti-Semitic Nazi propagandist he seems to be, or whether he "really" is a heroic American double agent risking his life every day to advance the Allied cause.

As Tony Tanner writes in his description of the novel, the problem is that "we may become our own cover-stories."[3] Almost every character in *Mother Night* has a cover, which masks his or her real identity. But by marvelous flights of sustained invention Vonnegut so mixes up these identities with accident, irony, and the pressures of history that the very fabric of individuality comes unraveled. At one point late in the novel Campbell is so disoriented by these shifts in identity that he finds himself standing stock still in Manhattan without the will to take another step, since he is unsure who is doing the stepping and for what purpose.

No one is who he or she seems in *Mother Night*. One of Campbell's Jewish prison guards had posed as a ruthless SS officer during the war in order to act as a double agent. While he succeeded in getting fourteen "innocent" SS men shot as suspected Allied spies, he was "such a pure and terrifying Aryan that they put me in a special detachment" (10). After the war, while Campbell is living anonymously in New York, he befriends a neighbor, George Kraft, who seems to be a painter but in fact is a Russian spy determined to kidnap Campbell and use him in Moscow's propaganda war against the United States. Even more disorienting is Campbell's reunion with his "wife" fifteen years after the war. He had presumed she had died entertaining troops at the Russian front, but is astonished and overjoyed to find a woman who appears to be his wife at his door, looking twenty years younger than she should. After making love with him, the woman confesses that she is not Campbell's wife, Helga, but Helga's younger sister, Resi. What she does not confess is that she is also a Russian spy, in league with Kraft. Though devastated by this revelation, in the end Campbell accepts the appearance for reality, since appearance is all he has: "God forgive me, I accepted Resi as my Helga" (104).

Part of the success of *Mother Night* is Vonnegut's ability to convey in it a depth of emotion he never achieved in his first two novels. While the horrors of totalitarianism in *Player Piano* and the threat of cosmic annihilation in *The Sirens of Titan* are dark enough subjects, those books fail to move the reader profoundly because of, respectively, wooden characterization and outlandishness. In an interview, when Robert Scholes said *Mother Night* was his favorite Vonnegut novel and praised its "dark" quality, Vonnegut agreed that it stands out from his other works up to that point because "it's more personally disturbing to me . . . because of the war and because of my German background."[4] In his introduction to the book Vonnegut wrote for the first time about Dresden—"the largest massacre in European history," which left its victims looking like "pieces of charred firewood two or three feet long" (vii)—and the novel itself contains a wrenching scene in a German bomb shelter in which Campbell watches the mother of several children come apart emotionally as "the big bombs walked all around above. And they walked and they walked and they walked, and it seemed they would never go away" (182). In *Mother Night*, then, Vonnegut was first coming to terms with the sources of what can only be called his essential pessimism—coming to terms with them not in an abstract, philosophical sense through the genre of sci-fi, but through the more direct medium of autobiographical fiction.

The book's pessimism extends from its title to its last page, when Campbell announces that he plans to kill himself. As Vonnegut, posing as the editor of Howard Campbell's confessions, points out, the title is from Goethe's *Faust*. It occurs in a passage in which Mephistopheles proclaims that "darkness gave birth to light"— in other words, that nonbeing is primary, being merely secondary. The passage from *Faust* Vonnegut quotes ends with Mephistopheles's wish that "it won't be long till light and the world's stuff are destroyed together" (xi). In his discussion of *Mother Night*, Mayo writes that "the world of Vonnegut's fiction is . . . constantly under the threat of annihilation."[5] Vonnegut's allusion to *Faust* makes clear that the threat comes not only from the man-made folly of war, but from the nature of the universe itself. For Vonnegut, as for many scientifically oriented writers of his generation such as Joseph Heller and Thomas Pynchon, the ultimate source of his pessimism is the principle of entropy—that over time complex systems fall apart. Much of Vonnegut's fiction is a restatement of an idea most powerfully set forth in the previous century by the philosopher Arthur Schopenhauer: that consciousness, the most complex of systems, itself may be a striking exception, an accidental and probably temporary anomaly in the vast unconscious process of the material universe. Against the background of such vast cosmic meaninglessness it is small wonder that so many of Vonnegut's characters consider suicide to hasten their inevitable return to the chilly embrace of Mother Night.

Yet *Mother Night* offers its compensations for this dark vision; if it did not, it never would have been appreciated by a popular audience. Its chief defense against despair, as elsewhere in Vonnegut's work, is humor. Vonnegut remarked in an interview that "the biggest laughs are based on the biggest disappointments and the biggest fears."[6] As Klinkowitz points out, in *Mother Night* "each character, and nearly every event, is structured as a three-part joke: premise, counter premise and, finally, solution in the form of a punchline."[7] The book's various spies at first seem to be one thing, then another, then neither—or both. For example, a Russian soldier loots Campbell's Berlin apartment and steals his manuscripts, then publishes them as his own after the war and becomes famous. Yet he gets in trouble not for plagiarism but for originality, because he writes his own satire of the Red Army after running out of Campbell's works and is tried and shot for treason. Likewise, Resi Noth at first appears as her sister Helga; then as herself, innocently in love; then as a Russian spy; and finally as a genuine lover who kills herself rather than lose Campbell. Many jokes depend on the reversal of expectations: prominent Nazis engage in Ping-Pong tournaments; Hitler loves Lincoln's Gettysburg Address; the notorious Adolph Eichman, writing his memoirs in prison in Israel, asks his fellow prisoner, "Do you think a literary agent is absolutely necessary?" Campbell replies, deadpan, "For book club and movie sales in the United States of America, absolutely" (128).

Finding humor in such grim subjects as the Holocaust and cosmic indifference to human concerns is characteristic of a "school" of American writing Bruce J. Friedman identifies in his book *Black Humor*. Friedman characterized black humor as a defining quality of postmodern American writers such as Terry Southern, John Barth, Joseph Heller, and Vonnegut. But Vonnegut traces black humor back further: "Freud had already written about gallows humor, which is middle-European humor. It's people laughing in the middle of political helplessness. . . . It's humor about weak, intelligent people in hopeless situations. And I have customarily written about people who felt there wasn't much they could do about their situations."[8] While the black-humorist tag would come to annoy Vonnegut, as had the sci-fi writer label, an awareness of the term is crucial in understanding the fusion of the tragic and comic sensibilities in his work. Significantly, Vonnegut's most famous phrase, one summing up the black humorist's fatalistic response to cosmic absurdity—"So it goes"—first appears in *Mother Night*.

Finally, *Mother Night* is superior to Vonnegut's earlier work because it extends the metafictional experiments of *The Sirens of Titan* and prepares the way for the radical self-reflexive quality of *Cat's Cradle*. Metafiction calls attention to its own artificiality in order to question the implicit claims of "realistic" writers that they are describing a stable world extant outside of language. Vonnegut subscribes to the postmodern ideas that one can know the world only through language; that linguistic systems are perpetually prone to arbitrariness, incoherence, and outright deceit; and that one alters that supposedly stable "outside" world simply by describing it. These ideas are the literary equivalent of Werner Heisenberg's uncertainty principle in physics, which notes that it is impossible to discover a particle's position and velocity at the same time, since the very act of observing these conditions alters them. In *Mother Night* linguistic systems range from the most idealistic to the most evil: from Campbell's romantic plays and erotic diary celebrating his marriage to Helga to the vile propaganda he turns out for the Nazis and to Eichman's memoirs, which seek to evade his responsibility for the murder of six million Jews. How does one sort out the real from the unreal, the truth from the deceit? As Tanner writes, "There is no cynical attempt to identify these two extreme ends of the spectrum, but it is part of Vonnegut's meaning to suggest that the artist cannot rest in confidence as to the harmlessness of his inventions."[9] Hitler uses the Gettysburg Address to celebrate fallen Nazis. Campbell's Russian plagiarist publishes Campbell's erotic diary as pornography—with illustrations.

Yet *Mother Night* celebrates the artist despite all this

CAT'S CRADLE

misuse of art. Having written nothing for years after the war, having become a "death worshipper" (36) after losing his wife, Campbell begins to recover when he buys a woodcarving set in 1958 and with it fashions a chess set from a broom handle in one sitting. This burst of pent-up energy and creativity leaves him with bloody hands but a lighter heart; looking for someone to share his accomplishment with, he makes his first friend (the spy, Kraft) since the war. When Helga/Resi shows up, he thinks for a time that she will inspire him to write again. If *Mother Night* prefigures *Jailbird* in terms of its being an account of the protagonist's crimes, it looks forward to *Bluebeard* as an acknowledgment of the interdependence and persistence against all odds of eros and art. Perhaps this is why Vonnegut ends the novel not with Campbell's threatened suicide, but with a question: "Auf wiedersehen?" Until we meet again?

Cat's Cradle

In *Cat's Cradle* (1963) Vonnegut hit full stride for the first time. In this jazzy, metafictional, Zen-influenced, mock-apocalyptic tour de force, he combined the tight control over his material afforded by the first-person point of view, which he had discovered in *Mother Night*, with the spectacular, zany inventiveness that distinguished *The Sirens of Titan*. The result was something new. In *The City of Words*, Tony Tanner describes much of postmodern American literature as the exploration of two conflicting views of the universe: that it is absolutely patterned or absolutely random, either of which in its pure form appears threatening. In *Cat's Cradle*, Tanner maintains, Vonnegut presents the reader with an alternative, "the idea of a pattern which is free form—something between utter shapelessness and absolute rigidity."[10] Like a good jazz composition Vonnegut's fourth novel is intricately patterned yet improvisational, intellectually demanding yet playful, "tight" yet free. Of course, to be this way is really the challenge of all groundbreaking art.

While *Mother Night*, with its World War II subject matter, had appealed to readers of Vonnegut's own generation, *Cat's Cradle* caught hold with a younger audience—the college crowd that would by the end of the decade make Vonnegut the most popular writer in America. Though still not widely known in the early 1960s Vonnegut was building up a cult following with his paperback sales that would soon explode into a publishing version of the Horatio Alger rags-to-riches story. As he explained in an interview, while he found it difficult early in his career not to have his work issued in hardcover or to be reviewed and treated seriously as a writer, being a paperback sci-fi/spy novelist did have its compensations: "I suppose it *was* a shame my books didn't come out in cloth, but a normal printing for a paperback was about 100,000 at the time and, if I had had the same work issued in hard-cover, I would have

been lucky to have reached a couple of thousand readers."[11] Paradoxically, by working in the popular forms
of genre fiction for a mass audience, Vonnegut prepared
the way for breaking out of the limitations of those
forms—and for teaching a generation of readers how to
perceive fiction in a new way.

The essence of that new way of reading is to undermine Coleridge's notion of "the willing suspension of
disbelief" on the part of the audience when experienc-
ing a literary work. In other words, rather than intentionally forgetting that what he is reading is unreal—the
pure invention of the writer—the reader of postmodern
writing should always be aware of that fact. To make
sure that he never forgets the writer constantly calls
attention to the artificiality of his art. Hence the first
sentence of *Cat's Cradle:* "Nothing in this book is true."
Vonnegut is of course aware of the logical paradox inherent in this assertion, for if the sentence itself is true,
then it negates itself. (If nothing in the book is true, and
the sentence is in the book, then the sentence itself is
not true; therefore, something *is* true in the book.) But
as he wrote in the 1966 introduction to *Mother Night,*
"Lies told for the sake of artistic effect . . . can be, in a
higher sense, the most beguiling forms of truth" (ix).

Cat's Cradle is a complete mythos of beguiling lies
ostensibly invented by one Lionel Boyd Johnson and
propagated by him on the Caribbean island of San
Lorenzo as the religion of Bokononism. Periodically the
narrator of the novel quotes from *The Books of Bokonon,*

explaining to the reader the religion's central terms and notions. Echoing the first sentence of the novel, *The Books of Bokonon*'s first sentence reads: "All of the true things I am about to tell you are shameless lies." The narrator then warns that "anyone unable to understand how a useful religion can be founded on lies will not understand this book [*Cat's Cradle*] either."[12] In Bokononism such useful lies are *foma*, or "harmless untruths . . . that make you brave and kind and happy." One key *foma* is the idea of a *karass*, which is a group of human beings organized into a team that does "God's Will without ever discovering what they are doing" (14). Contrasting with the meaningful *karass* is the insignificant *granfalloon*, or false *karass*, "a seeming team . . . meaningless in terms of the way God gets things done." Examples include "the Communist party, the Daughters of the American Revolution, the General Electric Company . . .—and any nation, anytime, anywhere" (82). Finally there is a *wampeter*, or "pivot of a *karass*" (50), the object around which the members of *karass* revolve "in the majestic chaos of a spiral nebula" (51). The *wampeter* of the narrator's *karass* is a new product of science—Ice-9. Invented by Dr. Felix Hoenekker, one of the "fathers" of the atomic bomb, Ice-9 effectively destroys life on earth at the end of the novel.

Cat's Cradle, then, is the story of two doomsday devices, either of which can lead the human race to the apocalyptic and it seems destined for throughout Vonnegut's fiction. The narrator announces early on that

CAT'S CRADLE

he had planned to collect material on the now-deceased Dr. Hoenekker for a book "limited to events that took place on August 6, 1945, the day the bomb was dropped on Hiroshima" (17). Writing to Hoenekker's son, Newton, the narrator asks for anecdotes that would help him "emphasize the *human* rather than the *technical* side of the bomb" (17). The narrator never actually completes *The Day the World Ended*, but the first half of *Cat's Cradle* consists of his gathering of information in the attempt to do so. The second part of this novel of two distinct halves concerns the narrator's unlikely journey to the island of San Lorenzo, where he learns of Bokononism and writes *Cat's Cradle* rather than his proposed book on Hoenekker and the bomb.

But who is this narrator, and why is he working on these projects? His first words are "Call me Jonah. My parents did, or nearly did. They called me John" (13). Jonah/John never gives himself a last name, and there is a sketchy, provisional quality to him that leads Richard Giannone to assert that "Jonah is not a character in the customary sense so much as he is a mock author. He is not a narrator with a personality developed from inherent qualities, for his several names [he says he could have been called Sam] tell us he is a reduction to narrative expedient."[13] The reader does learn that the narrator is a free-lance writer who smokes and drinks, who is separated from his wife, who is skeptical about the idea that advances in science will bring about a better world, and who is pessimistic but uses black humor to keep his despair from overwhelming him. In short, the narrator resembles his creator. At one point in *Cat's Cradle*, when John is taking a look at the graves of Dr. Hoenekker and his wife, he comes upon an unclaimed stone angel with the name of a "German immigrant" carved on it which "was my last name too" (66–67). Vonnegut says that he had originally identified the name as Vonnegut, but his editor convinced him to leave the name out since it was "just a bad idea."[14] Thus *Cat's Cradle* continues the autobiographical direction of Vonnegut's fiction that began with the satire of General Electric in *Player Piano*, appeared openly in his introduction to *Mother Night*, and would peak in the first and last chapters of *Slaughterhouse-Five*.

Vonnegut's narrator is autobiographical, but he is also richly allusive. As Giannone points out in an extended analysis of Vonnegut's opening allusion to *Moby-Dick* (the famous first line of which is "Call me Ishmael") and the book of Jonah in the Bible, Jonah/John presents a series of literary parallels that runs throughout the novel and gives coherence to its seeming vagaries of plot. Like Ishmael, who is the sole surviving witness of Captain Ahab's failed attempt to hunt down and kill the great white whale, Jonah/John is one of the few who remain alive after Ice-9 freezes the planet, and so he is "a spiritual Ishmael . . . who shadows forth the dire warning that we must change our ways if we are to avoid universal annihilation." Through his analysis of the novel's many allusions to the Jonah story Giannone concludes that Vonnegut implies "that science has led us so far astray that the enormous cry of Old Testament prophecy is needed to correct the course of life."[15]

In the first half of the book Vonnegut explores how science has led human beings to the point of destroying themselves. His portrait of Dr. Hoenekker is one of the most striking in his early fiction, for Vonnegut unexpectedly gives the reader not some sadistic, power-mad scientist but a mild, absent-minded professor with childlike curiosity. In an interview Vonnegut revealed that Hoenekker was based on the real-life scientist and Nobel Prize winner Irving Langmuir, who did research for GE before and during Vonnegut's years there. Vonnegut recalled that Languir was so absent-minded that he once "left a tip under his plate after his wife served him breakfast at home. I put that in [*Cat's Cradle*]. His most important contribution, though, was the idea for what I called Ice-9, a form of frozen water that was stable at room temperature."[16] Like his real-life model Dr. Hoenekker is totally out of touch with the real world, being completely consumed by his research. In the middle of his work on the atomic bomb he becomes interested in how turtles pull their heads in, and only gets back on track when agents of the Manhattan Project kidnap his turtles, leaving him nothing to do but return to nuclear physics.

But there is a dark side to Vonnegut's treatment of the stereotypical absent-minded professor. Hoenekker is a loveless man who pays no attention to his three

children, who would be a sad enough lot if they had
normally affectionate parents. Frank is a glum, uncom-
municative boy who spends his time building model
airplanes. Angela is a homely giant of over six feet who
had to drop out of school to take care of her father when
Mrs. Hoenekker died giving birth to Newt, a midget who
only got to play with his father once in his life. As Newt
says of his father in his letter to the narrator, "People
weren't his specialty" (24). Divorced from almost all human contact, Dr. Hoenekker plays with ideas as a child
plays with his companions. He produces the bomb as
casually as he makes a cat's cradle out of string—and
seems absolutely unaware of the moral consequences
for all mankind of his research. When one scientist expresses his fears that unleashing atomic power may be
a sin, Hoenekker blandly asks, "What is sin?"

This moral irresponsibility of scientists has been
one of Vonnegut's great themes from the beginning of
his career. In a recent interview he explained how his
experiences in World War II were a profound disillu-
sionment:

For me it was terrible, after having believed so much in
technology . . . to see the actual use of this technology
in destroying a city and killing 135,000 people and then
to see the even more sophisticated technology in the use
of nuclear weapons on Japan. I was sickened by this use
of the technology that I had had such great hopes for.
And so I came to fear it.[17]

61

CAT'S CRADLE

The second half of *Cat's Cradle* is Vonnegut's provisional psychic escape from the impossible situation in which human beings find themselves in the postnuclear age.

A weakness in *Cat's Cradle* is the shaky bridge that Vonnegut provides between the two major sections of the novel. In order to get John away from gathering information for *The Day the World Ended* at the lab at which Dr. Hoenekker had worked and to the island of San Lorenzo, Vonnegut treats himself to several unlikely coincidences. First, John by chance reads in the *New York Times* that Frank, whom he had presumed was dead, is actually alive and a member of the government of San Lorenzo. Next, John happens to get an assignment to write an article on a philanthropist living on the island. Finally, on the plane ride there he discovers Angela and Newt are his fellow passengers. All this is explained by the narrator's conversion to Bokononism, which casually accepts outrageous coincidences as the workings out of God's inscrutible will. As members of John's *karass* the others simply show up so as to move him closer to his *wampeter*, Ice-9.

The island of San Lorenzo is anything but a primitive, romantic escape from the horrors of the technological world: in fact it is infertile, impoverished, overpopulated, and run by a ruthless dictator, Papa Monzano. Vonnegut probably had in mind the similarly unfortunate Caribbean nation of Haiti, which is the poorest in the Western Hemisphere and which was run for decades by the notorious Papa Doc Duvalier and then for a time by his son, Baby Doc, before he was deposed. But as much as San Lorenzo resembles Haiti, Vonnegut's imaginary island owes perhaps more to Fidel Castro's Cuba. In 1962, when Vonnegut was at work on *Cat's Cradle*, the United States and the Soviet Union came close to war over the issue of nuclear missiles based in Cuba. The American naval blockade of the island and demand that the Russians remove their nuclear weapons marked the test of wills that became the definitive moment of the Cold War. Vonnegut was acutely aware of the crisis as he wrote, so that current historical events probably had as much to do with the novel's apocalyptic ending as did Vonnegut's awareness of such literary precursors as doomsday books like *On the Beach* and *Seven Days in May*.[18]

Once he gets John to San Lorenzo, in a parody of banana republic politics Vonnegut has John fall in love with Papa's beautiful daughter, then become president when Papa dies and Frank, like his father before him, refuses to take any responsibility. But the real business of the San Lorenzo section of the novel is to explore Bokononism. As much as anything *Cat's Cradle* is Vonnegut's application of the ideas he encountered as a graduate student in anthropology at the University of Chicago, the chief among them being the notion of cultural relativity. From this perspective people get caught up in the absurdities of *granfalloons* because they mistake their religion or nation as the *only* truth, when in fact there are many truths, or perhaps no truths. The central "truth" of Bokononism is that truth is provisional, not fixed. If Bokononism offers a higher truth than other religions, it is simply the open acknowledgment that it is all made up anyway. John learns that in the early days of the religion Johnson had teamed up with a man named McCabe and decided to outlaw Bokononism "in order to give the religious life of the people more zest, more tang" (143). While they failed to raise the standard of living on the island, the two rulers found that "as the living legend of the cruel tyrant in the city [McCabe] and the gentle holy man in the jungle [Johnson/Bokonon] grew, so too did the happiness of the people grow" (144). Here Vonnegut admits the truth of the classic Marxian formulation that religion is the opiate of the people—but with the twist that such opiates are necessary to deaden the pain of existence.

If science offers no cure-all for the human condition, however, neither does religion—not even of the enlightened Bokononist variety. Bokonon and McCabe eventually turn into their own personae, for even though "as young men, they had become pretty much alike, had both been half-angel, half-pirate, . . . the drama demanded that the pirate half of Bokonon and the angel half of McCabe wither away" (144). Soon McCabe is actually persecuting the Bokononists on the island, even putting them to death on "the hook"—this despite the fact that he is himself a Bokononist. Thus the two halves of *Cat's Cradle* show first science, then religion failing mankind. As Giannone writes, "Illium's affluence compensates for its spiritual poverty; San Lorenzo proffers spirituality to fill its material want. Together they school Jonah in the futility of aspiring to improve or even to understand the human condition."[19]

This bleak situation has its logical climax in the destruction of the world by Ice-9. John learns that each of the three Hoenekker children had gotten a piece of Ice-9 after their father's death, and, as Peter J. Reed writes, "all three end up buying love or a place of belonging with ice-nine. . . . One could almost say that the world ends because a father could not show his children love."[20] Newt had given over his Ice-9 to a Russian agent, a midget Ukrainian ballerina who claimed to love him; Angela had married a handsome industrialist who had courted her only for the enormous profits Ice-9 would bring him when he sold it to the US government; and Frank had bought his job on San Lorenzo by giving Ice-9 to Papa, who saw it as every petty dictator's dream—the ultimate weapon that could bring even the superpowers to their knees. But when the dying Papa commits suicide by swallowing Ice-9, and his body falls into the sea when a plane crashes into his castle, all the machinations of the characters for money, power, or love come to an end. The narrator and Mona temporarily escape to *Cat's Cradle*'s version of a fallout shelter— many Americans had such a shelter in their back yards in 1962—but they live in a nearly lifeless world where "it was winter, now and forever" (217). Here Vonnegut eerily anticipated the current speculations about a nu-

clear winter that could follow atomic warfare if the resulting dust blocked the sun's rays. Though John and
his beautiful companion have plenty of food to survive,
soon Mona commits suicide, suggesting the failure of
romantic love as a last defense against despair. John can
only quote the one-word chapter from *The Books of
Bokonon* entitled "What Can a Thoughtful Man Hope
for Mankind on Earth, Given the Experience of the Last
Million Years?" The chapter, in full, reads "Nothing"
(199).

Reed thus rightfully concludes that "*Cat's Cradle* is
more pessimistic even than *Mother Night*." It is also easy
to agree with his claims that, compared with the previous novel, the plot of *Cat's Cradle* "remains rather thin,
the characterizations are more superficial and often
fragmented, and the reader's involvement with characters, moral issues, and human emotions is consequently
shallower." But Reed counters his own criticism, however, with the recognition that "within the dimensions
of its chosen form, *Cat's Cradle* seems remarkably con-
sistent and to work well."[21] Vonnegut radically abandoned the representational novel for the first time in his
tale of Bokononism, and achieved his most striking
metafictional effects in it. Later experiments with the
self-reflexive mode, particularly *Breakfast of Champions*,
would prove less successful. But as distinctive as *Cat's
Cradle* is in Vonnegut's canon, its central concern of
exploring post-Christian ethics ties it to everything he
has written.

God Bless You, Mr. Rosewater

Of the three novels preceding *Slaughterhouse-Five*, *God Bless You, Mr. Rosewater* is unquestionably the least successful. Juxtaposed with the dazzling *Cat's Cradle*, it is a disappointment—less technically daring, containing characters developed at some length only to be abandoned, and finally guilty of sentimentality. Yet it is a worthwhile novel not only on its own modest merits but because it—along with *Mother Night*—marks the beginning of a significant change in Vonnegut's writing from a disposition toward fantasy to a growing devotion to realism. If *The Sirens of Titan*, despite its excesses, prepared the way for the imaginative flights of *Cat's Cradle*, *God Bless You, Mr. Rosewater* looks forward to the superior historical/political/social realism of *Jailbird*, *Deadeye Dick* and *Bluebeard*.

The premise of the novel is, quite simply, that America is an unjust society. The rich have convinced the majority of poor Americans that they deserve their poverty because they are lazy, stupid, spineless. So the rich get richer, and the poor lead lives of ever greater desperation. As Jerome Klinkowitz explains, there were autobiographical reasons for Vonnegut's choice of subject matter. He was in some of the worst financial circumstances of his life during this period: "His once reliable short-story market had disappeared completely, his novels produced but a meagre income, and his family life was rocky for a time."[22] Struggling to support six

GOD BLESS YOU, MR. ROSEWATER

children, apparently filed away as an inconsequential sci-fi writer by the critics, Vonnegut felt he was in danger of turning into his down-and-out doppelganger, Kilgore Trout. During this period, Klinkowitz writes, Vonnegut "came the closest ever to being Trout himself."[23]

It is small wonder that *God Bless You, Mr. Rosewater* begins, "A sum of money is a leading character in this tale about people, just as a sum of honey might properly be a leading character in a tale about bees."[24] The sum of money in question is over $87,000,000, the Rosewater family fortune. The Rosewaters' lawyers have placed it in the Rosewater Foundation in order to avoid taxes while still retaining control of the principal through the Rosewater Corporation. The Foundation has control of the Corporation's profits. As in a monarchy the presidency passes down the familial line to the closest relative upon the president's death. Eliot Rosewater, the novel's protagonist, is the Foundation's first president. Much of the book consists of the conflict between Eliot and his father, Senator Lister Rosewater, over what Eliot should do with his wealth. The senator is a social-Darwinist champion of capitalism; Eliot, to put it mildly, has other ideas.

In a marvelously biting letter written to his successor as president of the Foundation, which appears early in the novel, Eliot explains how the Rosewater fortune came about through greed, fraud, and bribery. Because the founding fathers set no limits on personal wealth, he explains, the real motto of the country became not *E pluribus unum* (out of many, one), but "Grab much too much, or you'll get nothing at all" (21). Because of the triumph of the robber baron mentality, the loading of the dice against the majority of Americans by the rich and their accomplices, the lawmakers and lawyers, "the American dream turned belly up, turned green, bobbed to the scummy surface of cupidity unlimited, filled with gas, went *bang* in the noonday sun" (21).

The visceral unpleasantness of this central image is characteristic of a generalized attraction/repulsion to the intimate functions of the human body running throughout the novel. Eliot himself is overweight, slovenly, fond of playing with his pubic hair, frequently drunk. His father, whose name sounds like a brand of mouthwash, is appalled by his son's personal habits. He offers a candid assessment of Eliot's altruism: "If Eliot's booze were shut off, his compassion for the maggots in the slime on the bottom of the human garbage pail would vanish" (59). Rotting corpses, garbage slime—such images proliferate in a novel in which, as Klinkowitz observes, "just about everything . . . is unpleasant."[25]

The ultimate source of the rot, however, is not physical but ethical, as Eliot's letter on the decay of the American dream suggests. While condemning the rapacious but heroic robber barons and their present-day heirs like Senator Lister, Vonnegut reserves special scorn for corporate underlings who weasel their way into wealth by unscrupulous means. The epitome of this sort is the vile lawyer Norman Mushari, who was hired by the Rosewaters' legal firm because its "operations could do with just a touch more viciousness" (17). Mushari seems an odd creation for a novelist who prides himself on never having created a villain, since he is absolutely without a redeeming trait. Vonnegut taunts him for being short, for being "the least Anglo-Saxon male member of the firm" (he is Lebanese), and for having "an enormous ass, which was luminous when bare" (17). Having observed Eliot's eccentric behavior, Mushari plans to get rich by proving he is insane and having the courts turn the Foundation over to Eliot's nearest relative, Fred Rosewater of Pisquontuit, Rhode Island. Elaborately set up early in the novel, Mushari fades in importance as it progresses, and so balances several characters introduced late in the narrative who do not provide enough formal or thematic justification for their existence.

Through Mushari, Vonnegut introduces Eliot's estranged wife, Sylvia, by having Mushari write to her requesting Eliot's letters, claiming that this is part of the normal procedure of divorce. Through this ruse Mushari becomes a voyeur peering into the most intimate details of the Rosewaters' lives. And as much as *God Bless You, Mr. Rosewater* is a story about money, it is also a story about love—or rather the failure of love. Eliot has failed Sylvia by frequently abandoning her for his hairbrained altruistic schemes—joining volunteer fire departments all over the country, showing up drunk at sci-fi conventions to praise the authors assembled there, exchanging his expensive clothes with bums on the street until his own closet is filled with smelly rags. But perhaps the greater failure is Sylvia's, because even though she is convinced that Eliot, despite his crazy behavior, is morally superior to the Musharis of the world, she is finally unable to follow his example. Under the pressure of the scorn of the rich for what she and Eliot are doing for the poor, she suffers a nervous collapse. Her psychiatrist coins a name for her new defense mechanism: "Samaritrophia . . . hysterical indifference to the troubles of those less fortunate than oneself" (54). Through this painful relationship Vonnegut suggests that a high moral calling many demand the sacrifice of normal family relationships—that a would-be saint may help strangers only to destroy the lives of those closest to him.

After separating from Sylvia, Eliot sets up shop over a liquor store in the run-down town of Rosewater, Indiana. The surrounding land has been strip mined, the town's main industries have shut down, and those who remain are the ignorant, the sick, the lonely. Vonnegut's Rosewater County is as full of eccentric losers as Nathanael West's southern California in *The Day of the Locust*. Eliot proclaims, "I'm going to love these discarded Americans—even though they're useless" (47). As the calls come in, Eliot answers each one with "Rosewater Foundation. How can we help you?" (49). When

GOD BLESS YOU, MR. ROSEWATER

people call threatening suicide, he offers to buy their lives for a few hundred dollars. Others call to tell their sad life stories or to complain about kidney ailments. Like a secular priest hearing confessions, Eliot listens patiently to these age-old complaints and offers what hope he can in the form of money, advice, or, most importantly, "uncritical love" (70).

Vonnegut has always been open to the charge of sentimentality in his writing—of dissolving into a river of uncritical love for dogs, children, the eccentric but lovable failure. At one point in *God Bless You, Mr. Rosewater*, after a particularly mournful conversation between Eliot and a despondent caller, Vonnegut seems to acknowledge he has gone too far by saying that "there was only the hopelessly sentimental music of the rainfall now" (74). But the presence of the hard-headed and hard-hearted Senator Lister in the novel shows how Vonnegut is willing to counter and even overthrow his own sentimentalizing tendencies. The senator is obviously flawed, yet Vonnegut lets him score a number of valid points against Eliot's gospel of uncritical love. His "Golden Age of Rome" speech in the Senate is a masterpiece of right-wing invective against society's weaklings. He makes the observation that his son has done very little in the long run for the poor by throwing money at them. But his most convincing argument is that Eliot's actions have cost him his wife and the children he might have had with her.

Like several of Vonnegut's novels—*Cat's Cradle* and

Jailbird spring to mind—*God Bless You, Mr. Rosewater* falls neatly into halves. Leaving Eliot in his office in Indiana, Vonnegut jumps to Rhode Island to tell the story of Eliot's nearest relative, Fred Rosewater, who is totally unaware that he stands to inherit a fortune if Eliot does not produce an heir. The son of a suicide, Fred sells insurance to his fellow poor on the hollow promise that they can become rich by dying. Hanging out in bars or sleeping on his boat in the afternoon, Fred leads an aimless life whose indirection is matched only by the aimlessness of Vonnegut's plotting in this part of the book. A rich lesbian idolized by Fred's wife, a homosexual restaurant owner who sells antiques, and a fisherman who is a parody of Hemingway are among a dozen or so characters Vonnegut introduces here but never satisfactorily integrates into the novel.

Finally getting back on his narrative track, Vonnegut has Fred come close to suicide before Mushari shows up with the news that he stands to inherit the Rosewater fortune. In this prince-and-the-pauper tale the prince has already taken on the pauper's rags; now the pauper seems about to become a prince. At this point Vonnegut switches back to conclude Eliot's story. After his father, unable to bear the sight of his dirty, drunken son any longer, denounces him as a failure, Eliot goes into a semicatatonic state in which he hardly recognizes his friends. Like Howard Campbell near the end of *Mother Night* he has simply lost the will to go on. One of his acquaintances in Rosewater observes that he has "clicked"—lost the driving force giving direction to his life. This mini-death of the psyche suggests that given the corruption of the world, anyone who tries to live morally may crack under the strain. Although he boards a bus out of town in order to meet Sylvia one last time in Indianapolis, there seems little reason to hope they have much of a chance for a reconciliation.

Like so many Vonnegut novels *God Bless You, Mr. Rosewater* ends, or at first appears to end, apocalyptically. Eliot's reading matter on the bus is Kilgore Trout's *Pan-Galactic Three-Day Pass,* which concerns an Earthling named Boyle who gets a surprise trip back home from his space mission to the end of the cosmos. Before he leaves, when he fearfully asks his commander whether a member of his family has died, the commander replies, "What's died, my boy, is the Milky Way" (199). Overwrought by Trout's grim novel and his own psychic collapse, as he enters Indianapolis Eliot hallucinates: "He was astonished to see that the entire city was being consumed by a fire storm" (200). Vonnegut shows just how close he was getting to being able to write *Slaughterhouse-Five* when he has Eliot recall a book called *The Bombing of Germany* that he has back in his office, which gives a graphic account of the destruction of Dresden. Historical fact (the bombing of Dresden), fiction (Eliot's hallucination of Indianapolis in flames), and metafiction (Trout's book on the destruction of the galaxy) merge in Rosewater's mind as one image of horror. As the imaginary fires rage, Eliot's world suddenly goes black.

Vonnegut rescues his novel from this disturbing end by having Eliot awake, in effect, in paradise. He comes to a year later in the garden of a mental hospital in Indianapolis, being attended to by the doctor who had treated his wife, by his family lawyer, by his father, and by Kilgore Trout. All the conflicts of the novel have been smoothed over, for Senator Lister and Trout—who should logically be at each other's throats—appear to be good friends in league to help Eliot prove at his hearing that he is not insane. Trout becomes Vonnegut's spokesperson, proclaiming that what Eliot did in Rosewater was "possibly the most important social experiment of our time." That experiment is to answer the question: "How to love people who have no use?" (210). In an obvious return to the concern about automation in *Player Piano*, Trout says that "we must find a cure" for the uselessness most Americans feel in a postindustrial age. Sounding more like a pop psychologist than the author of *Mouth Crazy*, Trout says that "people can use all the uncritical love they can get" (213). His last word, which seems wildly out of character, is "Joy" (214). All that is left is for Eliot to declare all the children of Rosewater County his heirs, and so invalidate the basis of Mushari's claim against him. Canceling out his imagined destruction of the world, Eliot ends with the hope that his adopted children will "be fruitful and multiply" (217).

God Bless You, Mr. Rosewater, then, is a flawed book with some merits. Written at a time of considerable fi-

GOD BLESS YOU, MR. ROSEWATER

nancial and emotional stress for Vonnegut, it reads like a cry from the heart rather than a novel under its author's full intellectual control. Its second half is clearly weaker than its first, a problem Vonnegut would continue to have to a lesser extent in *Jailbird* and *Deadeye Dick*. But in this book Vonnegut was beginning to write less about space travelers and more about his really central subject—ordinary Americans in sometimes extraordinary situations. Moreover, he was at this time gathering himself to write his most important novel.

Notes

1. *Mother Night* (New York: Delacorte/Lawrence, 1971) 21. Subsequent references are noted parenthetically.

2. Jerome Klinkowitz, *Kurt Vonnegut* (New York: Methuen, 1982) 51.

3. Tony Tanner, *City of Words* (New York: Harper, 1971) 187.

4. *Conversations with Kurt Vonnegut*, ed. William Rodney Allen (Jackson: University Press of Mississippi, 1988) 129. Hereafter *CKV*.

5. Clark Mayo, *Kurt Vonnegut: The Gospel from Outer Space* (San Bernardino: R. Reginald/Borgo Press, 1977) 26.

6. *CKV* 90.

7. Klinkowitz 49.

8. *CKV* 90–91.

9. Tanner 188.

10. Tanner 190.

11. *CKV* 200.

12. *Cat's Cradle* (New York: Delacorte/Lawrence, 1971) 16. Subsequent references are noted parenthetically.

UNDERSTANDING KURT VONNEGUT

13. Richard Giannone, *Vonnegut: A Preface to His Novels* (Port Washington, NY: Kennikat Press, 1977) 61.

14. *CKV* 205.

15. Giannone 54, 56.

16. *CKV* 182.

17. *CKV* 232.

18. Klinkowitz 52.

19. Giannone 62.

20. Peter J. Reed, *Kurt Vonnegut, Jr.* (New York: Warner, 1972) 142.

21. Reed 144–45.

22. Klinkowitz 58.

23. *Vonnegut in America*, ed. Jerome Klinkowitz and Donald L. Lawler (New York: Delacorte/Lawrence, 1977).

24. *God Bless You, Mr. Rosewater* (New York: Delacorte/Lawrence, 1971) 15. Subsequent references are noted parenthetically.

25. Klinkowitz, *Kurt Vonnegut* 58.

CHAPTER FOUR

Slaughterhouse-Five

Nearly a quarter of a century passed between the night Kurt Vonnegut survived the firebombing of Dresden in World War II and the publication of his fictionalized account of that event, *Slaughterhouse-Five*. As Vonnegut says, "It seemed a categorical imperative that I write about Dresden, the firebombing of Dresden, since it was the largest massacre in the history of Europe and I am a person of European extraction and I, a writer, had been present. I *had* to say something about it."[1] But the problem was, as Vonnegut remarks in the novel itself, "There is nothing intelligent to say about a massacre."[2] Consequently he was frustrated in his early attempts to tell the single story he felt he had to tell: "I came home in 1945, started writing about it, and wrote about it, and *wrote about it*, and WROTE ABOUT IT. . . . The book is a process of twenty years of this sort of living with Dresden and the aftermath."[3] Precisely because the story was so hard to tell, and because Vonnegut was willing to take the two decades necessary to tell it—to speak the unspeakable—*Slaughterhouse-Five* is

UNDERSTANDING KURT VONNEGUT

a great novel, a masterpiece sure to remain a permanent part of American literature.

The story of Dresden was a hard one for an American to tell for a simple reason: it was designed by the Allies to kill as many German civilians as possible, and it was staggeringly successful in achieving that aim. Because the government rebuffed his attempts shortly after the war to obtain information about the Dresden bombing, saying only that it was classified, it took Vonnegut years to realize the scale of the destruction of life on the night of February 13, 1945. What he eventually learned was that, by the most conservative estimates, 135,000 people died in the raid—far more than were killed by either of the atomic bombs the United States dropped later that year on Hiroshima and Nagasaki. Vonnegut was not killed himself in the attack by purest chance: he and a few other American POWs and their guards had available to them perhaps the only effective bomb shelter in the city, a meat locker two stories underground. They and only a handful of others survived the attack. This massive destruction of life was achieved by a technological breakthrough of sorts—the combination of two kinds of bombs that produced far greater devastation than either could have alone. As Vonnegut explained in an interview:

They went over with high explosives first to loosen things up, and then scattered incendiaries. When the war started, incendiaries were fairly sizeable, about as

long as a shoebox. By the time Dresden got it, they were
tiny little things. They burnt the whole damn town
down. . . . A fire storm is an amazing thing. It doesn't
occur in nature. It's fed by the tornadoes that occur in
the midst of it and there isn't a damned thing to
breathe. . . . It was a fancy thing to see, a startling thing.
It was a moment of truth, too, because American civilians and ground troops didn't know American bombers
were engaged in saturation bombing.[4]

In another interview he said, "When we went into the
war, we felt our Government was a respecter of life,
careful about not injuring civilians and that sort of
thing. Well, Dresden had no tactical value; it was a city
of civilians. Yet the Allies bombed it until it burned and
melted. And then they lied about it. All that was startling to us."[5]

Yet as crucial as Vonnegut's experience at Dresden
was to his life and his fictional career, he has resisted
the temptation to overdramatize it, to raise it to an
apotheosis of the sort Hemingway did of his wounding
in World War I at the Italian front. When asked if the
events at Dresden changed him, Vonnegut replied,
"No. I suppose you'd think so, because that's the cliché.
The importance of Dresden in my life has been consid-
erably exaggerated because my book about it became a
best seller. If the book hadn't been a best seller, it would
seem like a very minor experience in my life."[6] Dresden,
then, was no road-to-Damascus–like conversion to a to-

tally new way of thinking for Vonnegut; he was, after all, a young man convinced like most Americans of the necessity of destroying Nazism by whatever means necessary. The change came gradually, as a long process of thinking about the nature of war and writing about it, at first unsuccessfully. Finally, Vonnegut was less affected by the actual experience of Dresden than he would be by the fame that came with the enormous popularity of his book on the subject.

As James Lundquist puts it, Vonnegut's task in writing the novel was somehow to bridge "the increasing gap between the horrors of life in the twentieth century and our imaginative ability to comprehend their full actuality."[7] Indeed, what *can* one say about the madness in our time of human beings slaughtering their fellow human beings—coldly, methodically, scientifically, in numbers heretofore inconceivable? In his book *The Great War and Modern Memory*, Paul Fussell says that World War I was such a shock to those who experienced it that the only response they found adequate to describe it in literature was a searing irony. One thinks of such literary products of the war as Wilfred Owen's "Dulce et Decorum Est," a poem contrasting the martial phrase from Cicero that it is "sweet and proper" to die for one's country with the grotesque, panic-stricken death of soldiers in a mustard gas attack. But if World War I was a shock with its machine guns, its heavy artillery, and its trench-warfare charges into no-man's land, what of the next war with its saturation bombings,

SLAUGHTERHOUSE-FIVE

its death camps, its atomic bombs? Like the post–World War I writers Vonnegut had to find a new way to convey the horror, a new form to reflect a new kind of consciousness. He used irony, to be sure, but he went further, by altering the fundamental processes of narration itself. More than a conventional reminiscence of war, *Slaughterhouse-Five* is an attempt to describe a new mode of perception that radically alters traditional conceptions of time and morality.

Put most simply, what Vonnegut says about time in the novel is that it does not necessarily "point" only in one direction, from past to future. As Lundquist observes, "The novel functions to reveal new viewpoints in somewhat the same way that the theory of relativity broke through the concepts of absolute space and time."[8] Twenty years after the publication of *Slaughterhouse-Five*, theoretical physicists like Stephen F. Hawking are becoming more convinced that there is no reason why under some circumstances the "arrow of time" might point from future to past rather than from past to future.[9] If such a reversal is possible, then the famous description in *Slaughterhouse-Five* of a backwards movie (in which air force planes suck up bombs into themselves from the ground and fly backwards to their bases, where soldiers unload the bombs and ship them back to the factories to be disassembled) might be more than a wistful fantasy of a peaceful world. Of course, Vonnegut is less interested in new theories in physics than he is in his characters' confrontations with a world

UNDERSTANDING KURT VONNEGUT

that makes no sense in terms of their old ways of seeing it. Hence, rather than beginning his story by quoting Einstein, Vonnegut puts a particular person in a very particular situation: "Listen: Billy Pilgrim has come unstuck in time" (19).

But that striking opening sentence comes not in chapter 1 but in chapter 2. Chapter 1 consists of Vonnegut speaking in his own voice about the difficulties of writing *Slaughterhouse-Five*. Beginning with his 1966 introduction to the reissued *Mother Night*, Vonnegut had begun to speak more openly about himself and about the autobiographical connections underlying his writing. In the opening and closing chapters of *Slaughterhouse-Five*, however, he takes that process much further. By making the autobiographical "frame" of the novel part of the novel itself (rather than setting those sections apart as a preface and an afterword) Vonnegut, as Lundquist puts it, "conceptualizes his own life the way he later does Billy's, in terms of Tralfamadorian time theory. The structure of the chapter about writing the novel consequently prefigures the structure of the novel itself."[10] Vonnegut jumps from how he returned to Dresden in 1967 on a Guggenheim fellowship with his "old war buddy," Bernard V. O'Hare, to what it had been like to try to write about Dresden just after the war, to his first meeting after the war with O'Hare in Philadelphia, to his time teaching in the Writer's Workshop at the University of Iowa. Yet as Reed observes, "There is surprisingly little difficulty in following this seemingly disjointed narrative. The prologue [of] the first chapter, and the quick general guidelines to Billy's life in the second, provide the reader with a strong sense of direction from the outset."[11]

Perhaps most helpful is Vonnegut's discussion in chapter 1 of his failed attempts at writing a traditional narrative about Dresden—one with an Aristotelian beginning, middle, and end:

As a trafficker in climaxes and thrills and characterization and wonderful dialogue and suspense and confrontations, I had outlined the Dresden story many times. The best outline I ever made, or anyway the prettiest one, was on the back of a roll of wallpaper.

I used my daughter's crayons, a different color for each main character. One end of the wallpaper was the beginning of the story, and the other end was the end, and then there was all that middle part, which was the middle. And the blue line met the red line and then the yellow line, and the yellow line stopped because the character represented by the yellow line was dead. And so on. The destruction of Dresden was represented by a vertical band of orange cross-hatching, and all the lines that were still alive passed through it, came out the other side (4–5).

There are many reasons why such a traditional structure did not work for the novel Vonnegut wanted to write, but the principal one is that characters' lives, like those of real people, do not themselves proceed in one direction: in reality one does as much "backward" traveling in time through memory as "forward" traveling in anticipation of the future. Thus while not identical with it, *Slaughterhouse-Five*'s narrative mode is allied with the stream-of-consciousness technique pioneered by Joyce and Faulkner, which seeks to reproduce the mind's simultaneous blending of the past through memory, the present through perception, and the future through anticipation. Vonnegut's own life, and Billy Pilgrim's, is characterized by an obsessive return to the past. Like Lot's wife in the Bible, mentioned at the end of chapter 1, Vonnegut could not help looking back, despite the danger of being turned metaphorically into a pillar of salt, into an emblem of the death that comes to those who cannot let go of the past. To get to the heart of the matter of Dresden, moreover, Vonnegut felt he had to let go of the writer's usual bag of chronological tricks—suspense and confrontations and climaxes—and proceed by a different logic toward the future of the novel form.

Thus Vonnegut gives away what would be the traditional climax of his book—the execution of Billy's friend Edgar Derby "for taking a teapot that wasn't his"—in the novel's first paragraph. Throughout the novel he intentionally deflates suspense by mentioning in advance the outcome of any conflict he creates. The readers learn early, for example, that Billy will be kidnapped and taken to the planet Tralfamadore in 1967, where he will learn of the very different ways the Tralfamadorians view the universe. He learns as well that Billy will be shot to death on February 13, 1976, by Paul Lazzaro, a paranoid sadist Billy had been captured with in the war. He even learns with Billy the ultimate fate of the universe: the Tralfamadorians will accidently blow it up while experimenting with a new type of rocket fuel. Thus, rather than being like a straight line, the narrative chronology of *Slaughterhouse-Five* is more like an ascending, widening spiral that circles over the same territory yet does so from an ever higher and wider perspective. Finally, like most science fiction writers, Vonnegut hopes to push the reader's perceptual horizon as far as he can toward infinity—toward the union of all time and all space. There mystery remains, even though suspense disappears, since suspense is a function of a lack of knowledge at a single point in time and space.

Paradoxically, in creating this cosmic, nonlinear narrative Vonnegut uses fragments of all sorts of traditional narrative forms, much as a bird might use twigs, bits of string, and its own feathers to construct a nest, something very different than the sum of its parts. As Richard Giannone observes, "Graffiti, war memos, anecdotes, jokes, songs—light operatic and liturgical—raw statistics, assorted tableaux, flash before the reader's eye."[12] The most important linear narrative underlying all of these is the Judeo-Christian Bible, which is itself a central motif in *Slaughterhouse-Five*. There time proceeds from the creation to man's fall to the birth, crucifixion, and resurrection of Christ to the end of time with the Second Coming. Giannone suggests that the Gospels were "an amalgamation of language forms that were available to early Christians to spread their good tidings, rather than a fixed ideal shape sent down out of the blue. . . . [Yet] the old forms were inadequate to convey the momentous news, so primitive Christians made their own."[13] Thus Vonnegut tries in *Slaughterhouse-Five* to do what the Gospel writers attempted to do in their time: construct a new form out of the fragments of old forms.

That Vonnegut was conscious of doing so—that he found the Christian, linear vision of time no longer adequate—is apparent by his remarks in the novel on a book by Kilgore Trout called *The Gospel from Outer Space.* According to Trout, the traditional Gospels are flawed because they seem to suggest that the moral lesson one should learn from Jesus' crucifixion is: *"Before you kill somebody, make absolutely sure he isn't well connected."* In Trout's revised version of the story, rather than being the Son of God, "Jesus really *was* a nobody, and a pain in the neck to a lot of people with better connections than he had. He still got to say all the lovely and puzzling things he said in the other Gospels" (94). Yet when this nobody is crucified, the heavens open up with thunder and lightning, and God announces that he *"will punish horribly anybody who torments a bum who has no connections"* (95). In the course of the novel it becomes clear that the weak, hapless, clownishly dressed Billy

Pilgrim is precisely this "bum who has no connections"—that he is in effect a sort of new Christ. Such
observations as the fact that Billy lay "self-crucified"
(69) on a brace in his German POW boxcar, or that Billy
"resembled the Christ of the carol" (170) that Vonnegut
takes as the novel's epigraph ("The cattle are lowing, /
The baby awakes. / But the little Lord Jesus / No crying
he makes.") make clear that this identification of Billy
as a Christ-figure is Vonnegut's conscious intention.

Like Christ, Billy brings a new message to the
world, although it is a very different one from his predecessor's. And like Jesus he is an innocent who accepts
his death, at the hands of an enemy who reviles and
misunderstands him, as an opportunity to teach mankind the proper response to mortality. Both Billy and
Jesus teach that one should face death calmly, because
death is not the end. In the Christian vision the self after
death proceeds forward in time eternally, either in
heaven or hell; for Billy, however, "after" death the soul
proceeds backward in time, back into life. As Billy
learns from the Tralfamadorians,

When a person dies he only *appears* to die. He is still
very much alive in the past, so it is very silly for people
to cry at this funeral. All moments, past, present, and
future, always have existed, always will exist. The Tralfamadorians can look at all the different moments just
the way we can look at a stretch of the Rocky Mountains, for instance. They can see how permanent all the

moments are, and they can look at any moment that interests them. It is just an illusion we have here on Earth that one moment follows another one, like beads on a string, and that once a moment is gone it is gone forever (23).

Thus Billy, the new Christ, preaches that human beings *do* have eternal life—even if there is no life after death.

The literary consequence of the Tralfamadorian conception of time is the Tralfamadorian novel, which consists of "brief clumps of symbols read simultaneously." As the Tralfamadorians tell Billy, these symbols, or messages, when seen all at once "produce an image of life that is beautiful and surprising and deep. There is no beginning, no middle, no end, no suspense, no moral, no causes, no effects" (76). *Slaughterhouse-Five* is of course itself an attempt to write this sort of book, as Vonnegut announces in his subtitle: "This is a novel somewhat in the telegraphic schizophrenic manner of tales of the planet Tralfamadore." While human beings cannot read all the passages of the book simultaneously, its short length, its scrambled chronology, its deft juxtapositionings of different times to make thematic points, and its intricate patterns of imagery all combine to give the reader something of that effect. Once he finishes the novel—after a few hours, perhaps in one sitting—the reader can visualize all of Billy's moments stretched out before him like the Rocky Mountains; further, he can see the author's life in the same way, all the way from

SLAUGHTERHOUSE-FIVE

World War II to the assassination of Robert Kennedy in 1968, when Vonnegut was composing the last pages of *Slaughterhouse-Five*.

Yet while the novel boldly attempts to do away with traditional chronological narration on one level, it still gives the reader a story that builds toward the bombing of Dresden, which is recounted in greatest detail late in the book. Rather than being a traditional novel or a purely experimental, "Tralfamadorian" novel, *Slaughterhouse-Five* is more like one superimposed on the other. One can easily follow the traditional *Bildungsroman* of Billy's life. Born in 1922, like his creator, he endured a childhood marked by intense fears— of drowning when his father subjected him to the "sink or swim method," of falling into the Grand Canyon on a family trip, of the total darkness when the guides extinguished the lights in Carlsbad Caverns. These early images have great relevance for Billy's fear and ineptitude in the war and afterward. His refusal to try to swim and consequent passive sinking to the bottom of the pool is a symbolic wish to return to the safety of the womb. Billy falls constantly in the novel—into ditches, from boxcars, from the sky in a plane crash— despite his intense fear of falling epitomized by his Grand Canyon experience. Finally, the darkness in Carlsbad Caverns prefigures that in the meat locker two stories underground in Dresden—the most important symbolic womb into which Billy retreats for safety. One of the many ironies of the book is that such a passive person should be one of the few to survive the destruction of the city. As Vonnegut says simply of his hero, "He was unenthusiastic about living" (52).

After this shaky childhood Billy attends college for only a few weeks before going off to war as an unarmed chaplain's assistant. In no time he is captured, along with a hapless tank gunner named Roland Weary, in the Battle of the Bulge, the last great German counteroffensive of the war. Freezing in inadequate clothing, hungry, frightened out of his wits, Billy becomes "unstuck in time" for the first time, finding himself living moments out of his past or his future. Weary dies in transit to the POW camp of gangrene of the feet, which he had claimed was caused when the time-tripping Billy abstractedly stepped on him. Before he dies, Weary tells his story to Paul Lazzaro, who vows to avenge Weary's death by tracking Billy down after the war and killing him. Lazzaro is an emblem of the fact that a soldier can never really escape his war experiences—that they will always "track him down" even years later. In the POW camp the dispirited group of Americans is greeted by some hale and hearty Englishmen who have been there most of the war, growing healthy on good Red Cross food (sent by mistake in excessive amounts), exercise, and English optimism. They are the opposite of Billy, the fatalistic, disheveled weakling who simply drifts from one disaster to the next in helpless resignation. After a falling out with the Englishmen over personal hygiene and philosophical attitudes, the Americans are

SLAUGHTERHOUSE-FIVE

sent to Dresden, a supposedly "open" city, where they soon have their rendezvous with the most significant day in the city's history, February 13, 1945.

After the war Billy does far better than one would expect, since he becomes an optometrist, marries the boss's daughter, and is soon driving a Cadillac, living in an all-electric home, and pulling in over $60,000 a year. But the thematic reason Vonnegut makes Billy so successful is perhaps more important than the slight problem of verisimilitude: Vonnegut wants to show that all Billy's material comforts—his magic fingers bed, the expensive jewelry he gives Valencia, his wife, his fancy car (which will be the cause of his wife's death)—can do nothing to smooth over the pain of what he has experienced. Shortly after the war Billy had checked himself into a mental hospital, where he received shock treatments for depression. Today his problem would be called posttraumatic stress syndrome. Late in the novel, as he feels agony while listening to a barbershop quartet sing "That Old Gang of Mine" at a party celebrating his wedding anniversary, Billy realizes that "he had a great big secret somewhere inside," even though "he could not imagine what it was" (149). His secret is of course the awareness of the horrors of war and the certainty of death—an awareness the frantic material-ism of postwar America was desperately trying to cover up.

The cracks in the American dream show through Billy's apparently successful postwar life. Valencia is a parody of consumerism, since she constantly consumes candy bars while making empty promises to lose weight in order to please Billy sexually. Billy's son appears to be headed for jail as a teen-ager before he joins the Green Berets and goes off to fight in Vietnam. On his way to the office Billy stops at a traffic light in a burned-out ghetto area and drives away when a black man tries to talk with him. Vonnegut was obviously responding to the incredible social tensions of the late 1960s, which saw the burning of major portions of several American cities in race riots, the assassinations of John F. Kennedy, Martin Luther King, Jr., and Robert Kennedy, and the seemingly endless acceleration of the war in Vietnam. A major reason *Slaughterhouse-Five* had the enormous impact it did was because it was published at the height of the conflict in Vietnam, and so delivered its antiwar message to a most receptive audience. In a book of powerful passages, there is no more powerful one than this at the end of the novel, in Vonnegut's autobiographical chapter 10: "Robert Kennedy, whose summer home is eight miles from the home I live in all year round, was shot two nights ago. He died last night" (182). One of Robert Kennedy's promises in his presidential campaign was to stop the war, and when he died that hope seemed to die with him. For Vonnegut, and for Billy, it must have seemed that Dresden was happening all over again in Vietnam.

In 1967, on the night of his daughter's wedding, Billy is picked up by a flying saucer and taken in a time

warp to Tralfamadore, where he is displayed in a sort
of Tralfamadorian zoo by his abductors. Since Billy had
not been very happy on earth, he finds that during his
stay of several years (in terms of Tralfamadorian time,
not Earth time) he is "about as happy as I was on Earth"
(98). His happiness is increased when the Tralfamadorians kidnap a sexy movie actress, Montana Wildhack,
and bring her to the zoo as Billy's "mate." So while Billy
enjoys sexual bliss for the first time with the willing Ms.
Wildhack, he gets instruction from the Tralfamadorians
on the true nature of the universe. Billy and Montana
appear as a sort of new Adam and Eve, who live in the
confines of a perfect world, until Billy eats from the tree
of knowledge, in effect, by learning the true nature of
time and the place of conscious beings in the universe.
He is expelled from his symbolic garden when the Tralfamadorians (for unexplained reasons) send him back
to Earth. An enlightened Billy then begins his mission
of preaching his new gospel to his fellowmen—who are
understandably skeptical about his claims.

Vonnegut leaves room for the idea that Billy's trip
to Tralfamadore is all in Billy's mind. This sort of "escape hatch" from fantasy into realism is characteristic
of the sci-fi genre: in *A Connecticut Yankee in King
Author's Court* Twain has his hero receive a blow on the
head and probably dream the novel's events. In *Slaughterhouse-Five* Billy had been in a mental hospital and
received shock treatments. During his stay there he had
met Eliot Rosewater, who makes a cameo appearance

from Vonnegut's previous novel in order to introduce
Billy to the sci-fi works of Kilgore Trout. One of the
novels Billy reads, *The Big Board*, concerns an Earth couple kidnapped by aliens and displayed on their planet
in a zoo. An event in 1968, moreover, suggests a physical explanation for the Tralfamadorian episodes: Billy
survives a plane crash on the way to an optometrists'
convention that kills everyone else and leaves him with
a serious head injury. In chapter 1 of the novel Vonnegut mentions the French writer Céline, who had received a head wound fighting in World War I, and who
had thereafter heard voices and had written his death-
obsessed novels during his sleepless nights. Like Billy,
Céline too was obsessed with time: Billy's Tralfamadore
experience may be seen as the equivalent of Celine's—
and Vonnegut's—attempts to deal with the problem of
mortality through writing fiction. As Vonnegut observes of Rosewater and Billy, "They had both found
life meaningless, partly because of what they had seen
in war. . . . So they were trying to re-invent themselves
and their universe. Science fiction was a big help" (87).

Billy's trip to Tralfamadore, then, finally begins to
look more like a metaphor than a literal description of
events. His space travel is simply a way for Vonnegut
to describe the growth of his own imagination out of the
Christian, linear vision of time to the cosmic perspective
of time as the fourth dimension. This is not to say, however, that Vonnegut offers the Tralfamadorian *attitudes*
toward that vision as final truth. Tralfamadorians—

"real" or imagined—are not human beings, so that their attitude of absolute indifference toward the terrors of the universe—even to the ultimate terror of its annihilation—could never work for humans. If *Slaughterhouse-Five* is a combination of the traditional narrative and the Tralfamadorian novel, it is also a synthesis of Christian and Tralfamadorian morals: the reader is not so much urged to choose the latter over the former as to superimpose the two. When Billy passionately implores the Tralfamadorians to tell him how they live in peace, so that he can return to give that knowledge to Earth, his hosts reply that war and peace come and go at random on Tralfamadore as they do everywhere else. Their response to any frustration on Billy's part—to his profoundly human need to know why—is simply that "there is no *why*" (66). When Billy wonders why the universe must blow up, they respond that "the moment is structured that way." The Tralfamadorians claim that "only on Earth is there any talk of free will" (74). Such profound indifference could never suffice for human beings, nor does Vonnegut imply that it should.

Slaughterhouse-Five is built on the paradox that it appears to offer acceptance and even indifference as responses to the horrors of the twentieth century, when in fact it is a moving lament over those horrors—a piercing wail of grief over the millions of dead in World War II. Emblematic of this paradox is a short phrase from the novel that has become probably the best-known and most often repeated by his readers of any in Vonnegut's

UNDERSTANDING KURT VONNEGUT

work: "So it goes." In *Palm Sunday* Vonnegut explains that the phrase was his response to his reading of Céline's *Journey to the End of Night*: "It was a clumsy way of saying what Céline managed to imply . . . in everything he wrote, in effect: 'Death and suffering can't matter nearly as much as I think they do. Since they are so common, my taking them so seriously must mean that I am insane.' "[14] Every time someone dies in the novel—from Wild Bob to Valencia to Billy Pilgrim himself to Robert Kennedy—Vonnegut repeats "So it goes." Once this pattern is established, Vonnegut has fun with it, as when he has Billy pick up a bottle of flat champagne after his daughter's wedding: "The champagne was dead. So it goes" (63). Thus the phrase finally embodies all the essential attitudes toward death in the novel—acceptance, sorrow, humor, outrage. If at times "So it goes" reads like a resigned "Let it be," it more often comes through as the reverse: "Let it be *different*—let all these dead live!" So Vonnegut does let them live, in effect, by positing the Tralfamadorian idea that they are always alive in their pasts.

Despite its mask of Tralfamadorian indifference *Slaughterhouse-Five* conveys at times an almost childlike sense of shock that the world is such a violent place. Children form an important motif in the book, which is subtitled "The Children's Crusade." Vonnegut had chosen that ironic phrase as a way to reassure Mary O'Hare, Bernard's wife, that he was not going to portray war as a glamorous affair fought by "Frank Sinatra

SLAUGHTERHOUSE-FIVE

and John Wayne or some of those other glamorous war-loving, dirty old men" (13). When the British POWs, after several years in captivity, see Billy and the other recently captured Americans, they confess that "we had forgotten that wars were fought by babies" (91). Before recounting the bombing of Dresden, Billy and his young German guard see a group of adolescent girls taking a shower. They are "utterly beautiful" (137). Yet when the bombs begin to fall, Vonnegut records that "the girls that Billy had seen naked were all being killed. . . . So it goes" (152).

But *Slaughterhouse-Five* does not stop with the pathos of innocent children being killed. It refuses to be a self-satisfied antiwar book like, say, *Johnny Got His Gun*. While conveying a sense of outrage, horror, regret, and even despair over the insanity of war, Vonnegut does not think that stopping war is a realistic possibility or that, if it were, this would end the pain of the human condition. In chapter 1, when talking about his Dresden project to a movie producer, Vonnegut had gotten the response, " 'Why don't you write an anti-*glacier* book instead?' What he meant, of course, was that there would always be wars, that they were as easy to stop as glaciers. I believe that, too" (3). Even more significant is Vonnegut's admission that "if wars didn't keep coming like glaciers, there would still be plain old death" (3). Finally, while Vonnegut accepts war and death as inevitable, he refuses to endorse the sentimentalized, childlike attitude of acceptance of the inevitable epitomized in the prayer hanging on Billy's office wall and inside a locket on a chain hanging around Montana Wildhack's neck: "God grant me the serenity to accept the things I cannot change, courage to change the things I can, and wisdom always to tell the difference" (52, 181). As Vonnegut observes, "Among the things Billy Pilgrim could not change were the past, the present, and the future" (52). Dresden has happened, is happening, and will always happen.

Yet if the war is always going on, it is always ending, too. Life comes out of death, as surely as Billy survives the bombing of Dresden in a slaughterhouse. In chapter 1 Vonnegut describes the end of the war, when thousands of POWs of all nationalities were gathered in a beetfield by the Elbe River. This moment of liberation of the soldiers of all countries would grow for twenty years in Vonnegut's mind until it became the central image in *Bluebeard*, his most recent novel. The last sound in *Slaughterhouse-Five* is not that of bombs falling, but of a bird chirping just after the war: *"Poo-Tee-weet?"* By making the chirp a question Vonnegut seems to ask all the survivors of the war, "Despite everything, would you like to try again?"

Reed speaks for most critics of Vonnegut's writing when he says, that *"Slaughterhouse-Five* remains a remarkably successful novel ... [that] neither falters from, nor sensationalizes the horrors it depicts, and tenaciously avoids pedantic or moralistic commentary; no small achievement given the subject matter and the author's personal closeness to it."[15] Vonnegut was indeed close to the events of *Slaughterhouse-Five*, but it took him nearly a quarter of a century to get far enough away from them in time to have the proper perspective. The authority of that perspective perhaps most forcefully rings through the simple phrase Billy utters about Dresden near the novel's end: lying in his hospital bed after his plane crash, listening to Bertrand Rumfoord belittle the "bleeding hearts" who would mourn the loss of innocent life in the Allied firebombings, Billy responds: "I was there" (165). Finally, *Slaughterhouse-Five* gains its power not as an act of moralizing, but of witness.

Notes

1. *Conversations with Kurt Vonnegut*, ed. William Rodney Allen (Jackson: University Press of Mississippi, 1988) 230. Hereafter *CKV*.
2. *Slaughterhouse-Five* (New York: Delacorte/Lawrence, 1969) 17. Subsequent references are noted parenthetically.
3. *CKV* 163.
4. *CKV* 173–74.
5. *CKV* 95.
6. *CKV* 94.
7. James Lundquist, *Kurt Vonnegut* (New York: Ungar, 1976) 69.
8. Lundquist 71.
9. Stephen F. Hawking, *A Brief History of Time* (New York: Bantam, 1988).
10. Lundquist 75.

11. Peter J. Reed, *Kurt Vonnegut, Jr.* (New York: Warner, 1972) 179.

12. Richard Giannone, *Vonnegut: A Preface to His Novels* (Port Washington, NY: Kennikat Press, 1977) 84.

13. Giannone 85–86.

14. *Palm Sunday* (New York: Delacorte/Lawrence, 1981) 296.

15. Reed 203.

CHAPTER FIVE

Breakfast of Champions; Slapstick

As the 1970s began, despite the enormous success of *Slaughterhouse-Five*—a success compounded by the release in 1972 of an excellent film based on the novel—Vonnegut felt that he had come to the end of one part of his life and found himself not knowing exactly what to do next:

Well, I felt after I finished *Slaughterhouse-Five* that I didn't have to write at all anymore if I didn't want to. It was the end of some sort of career. . . . So I had a shutting-off feeling, you know, that I had done what I was supposed to do and everything was OK. And that was the end of it. I could figure out my missions for myself after that.[1]

He had written the book he had to write, and he naturally felt the simultaneous sense of release and depression one often feels after finally achieving a lifelong goal. All his books were now selling phenomenally well; he could live comfortably off his royalties for the foreseeable future. Yet ironically, at the height of his success Vonnegut was entering into perhaps the most emotionally trying period of his life. Worn out by the turbulent times and advancing age, seeing his children leave home for communes and colleges, he found his marriage of twenty-five years on the rocks. As he writes in *Palm Sunday*, "It was a good marriage for a long time—and then it wasn't."[2] For a native midwesterner from a family in which divorce was virtually unheard of, the breakup was a source of great confusion and embarrassment. But in 1971 Vonnegut moved out of the family house on Cape Cod and came alone to New York City to begin a new stage of his life.

Like many recently divorced people he found his new situation anything but liberating. Rather than being the story of "booze and wicked women," Vonnegut confesses, his early years in New York were "a tale of a man's cold sober flight into unpopulated nothingness."[3] He became so depressed that he was put on medication by his physician. In 1972 his son Mark had a schizophrenic breakdown and had to be hospitalized, further distressing Vonnegut with guilt and fear that he himself might have a genetic predisposition to insanity. It is hardly surprising that his next novel would offer the hypothesis that human beings are at the mercy of the chemical compositions of their brains. As he admits in *Palm Sunday*, during that tremendously difficult time he considered suicide: "It has always been a temptation to me, since my mother solved so many problems with

BREAKFAST OF CHAMPIONS

it. The child of a suicide will naturally think of death . . . as a logical solution to any problem."[4] Given these grave psychic conflicts, it is a wonder that Vonnegut managed to write anything at all during these years.

Breakfast of Champions

The wonder is even greater that *Breakfast of Champions* (1973), despite its considerable flaws, is as good a novel as it is. The full toll of his personal problems on Vonnegut's writing would only appear in *Slapstick,* a failed book by any standards. *Breakfast of Champions* occasionally shows some of the spark of *Slaughterhouse-Five*, and so in effect looks backward to Vonnegut's major phase. In fact, much of the matter of *Breakfast of Champions* had originally been in Vonnegut's Dresden novel. As he recalled in an interview, "*Slaughterhouse-Five* and *Breakfast* used to be one book. But they just separated completely. It was like a pousse-café, like oil and water—they simply were not mixable. So I was able to decant *Slaughterhouse-Five*, and what was left was *Breakfast of Champions*."[5] But Vonnegut had reservations about what was left over from the decanting. In 1971 he said he was giving up on the new book because "it was a piece of ————."[6] When the novel finally appeared after Vonnegut changed his mind and finished it, it contained several disclaimers as to its literary merit. In his preface he writes, "What do I myself think of this particular book? I feel lousy about it, but I always feel lousy about my books."[7] Later in the novel Vonnegut is more pointed: " 'This is a very bad book you're writing,' I said to myself" (198).

Breakfast of Champions is a better effort than its author gives it credit for being, but its problems are still serious ones. Perhaps the most immediately apparent is the lack of a sufficiently dramatic center to hold together all the disparate events of the novel. As Vonnegut himself admits in his preface, "This book is a sidewalk strewn with junk" (6). *Slaughterhouse-Five* consists of many fragments, but they all come together to point toward a crucial moment in history: the bombing of Dresden. *Breakfast of Champions* has no such dramatic center. In fact, its climax is the deliberately farcical meeting up of a Pontiac salesman named Dwayne Hoover, Kilgore Trout, and Kurt Vonnegut himself in a Holiday Inn in Midland City, Indiana. A fight breaks out, but it is treated in intentionally anticlimactic terms. The real interest in the novel is not so much the literal action as it is the way Vonnegut comments on that action so as to reveal his concerns about the nature of writing, the strained social fabric of American society, and the tenuous state of his own psyche. As Vonnegut has himself say to a waitress at the Holiday Inn who asks whether he can see in the darkness with the sunglasses he is wearing, "The big show is inside my head" (206). Some critics have argued that this is exactly the problem: *Breakfast of Champions* is a solipsistic bit of fun

BREAKFAST OF CHAMPIONS

on its author's part that never connects meaningfully either with the "real" world or with its readers.

The novel does carry the metafictional impulse in Vonnegut's writing as far as it can go, to the point of the author's appearing in the novel, as himself, and even talking to his fictional alter ego, Kilgore Trout, and finally setting him free. This action seems to reflect Vonnegut's sense that he had come to the end of the first half of his career and that it was time to move on. If Kilgore Trout represented the down-and-out, seldom-read sci-fi writer Vonnegut had feared in the early 1960s he could become, then it would seem logical that the wildly popular and financially secure Vonnegut of the 1970s could feel confident enough to let that image of himself go. But Trout would not die so easily, and would make a reappearance in Vonnegut's subsequent novels. He returns because of a persistent sense of insecurity in Vonnegut about his status as a serious writer, an intellectual worthy of a sophisticated audience. As Vonnegut confesses in his preface, "I have no culture, no humane harmony in my brains. I can't live without a culture anymore" (6). The effect of all this confession in *Breakfast of Champions*, however, is somewhat disconcerting, like overhearing someone talking to himself or herself about painful personal matters. As Peter Reed characterizes it, "Vonnegut's projection of self into this novel is such that the reader finds it hard to escape the sense that *Breakfast of Champions*, at least in the later chapters, is personal in a rather exclusive way. . . . The effect results in the reader's feeling partially estranged in the fictional world into which he has apparently been invited."[8]

What Vonnegut was confessing in *Breakfast of Champions*, perhaps more to himself than to the reader, was not so much that he feared he might be a bad writer as that he no longer had much will to live. As he admitted, "Suicide is at the heart of the book. It's also the punctuation mark at the end of many artistic careers. I pick up that punctuation mark and play with it in the book, come to understand it better, put it back on the shelf but leave it in view."[9] As the son of a melancholy father who saw his career disintegrate in the Depression, and of a depressed mother who finally killed herself with sleeping pills, Vonnegut has had to struggle against a heritage of despair. *Breakfast of Champions* is an account of that struggle told at times in fictionalized terms, at times in directly autobiographical ones. Near the center of the novel Dwayne Hoover could be speaking for his creator when he cries out, "I've lost my way. . . . I need somebody to take me by the hand and lead me out of the woods" (171). In this possible allusion to Dante's *Divine Comedy*, Vonnegut expresses his anguish at being in the dark night of the soul—lost in the metaphoric woods of the middle of life's journey. The last image in the book is a self-portrait of Vonnegut with a tear falling from his eye. The emotional pain of *Breakfast of Champions* is almost palpable, and makes it a tremendously revealing but difficult book to read.

BREAKFAST OF CHAMPIONS

A casual glance at the book might suggest the opposite, for it seems to be filled with cartoons. Taking the perspective of someone who must explain *everything*, Vonnegut draws pictures for his readers—of a chicken, a cow, a hamburger, a Holiday Inn, and, most infamously, of his rectum. As he excuses himself in his preface, "I am programmed at fifty to perform childishly—to insult "The Star Spangled Banner," to scrawl pictures of a Nazi flag and an asshole and a lot of other things with a felt-tipped pen" (5). Many readers and critics were offended by what they saw as a juvenile and prurient streak in Vonnegut manifested by these drawings. But Vonnegut's purpose is not to titillate but to allow the reader to see through convention. Klinkowitz says of the drawings, "We are at once reminded of the simple essence of a thing, and also of its inexorability. *There it is,* says the text, in a manner so plain that we are forced to see what rhetoric and myth obscures."[10] By drawing what he sees on the "sidewalk strewn with junk" of American culture, Vonnegut holds up to scrutiny the objects that define the American character in often unflattering ways—skid row signs, guns, electric chairs, bombs.

Like all of Vonnegut's novels *Breakfast of Champions* is an exposé of the flaws in a society supposedly dedicated to providing freedom and justice for all. The American landscape through which the characters move has been polluted, strip mined, and made horrifically ugly with advertisements of all kinds. Seemingly everything in the novel is plastered with a sign of some sort: people wear T-shirts with inane slogans and buttons with smiley faces or come-ons for the Arts Festival at Midland City; trucks scream out their companies' names in letters eight feet high; and the roadsides are disfigured with everything from encouragements to "Visit Miracle Cave" to hand-lettered signs warning blacks to stay out of town. The novel's title itself comes from the advertising slogan of a breakfast cereal. For the former public relations man for General Electric, truth in advertising is an oxymoron. Vonnegut's grim vision is of a country frantically on the move, its acquisitive impulses directed by amoral corporations toward the consumption of products that are at best worthless and at worst actively harmful.

Vonnegut deals with this part of the novel—the critique of American culture—chiefly through the journey of Kilgore Trout from New York to Midland City. Through the intervention of Eliot Rosewater, his single fan, Trout has been "discovered" and invited to participate in Midland City's Arts Festival. Trout perversely decides to attend "to show them what nobody has ever seen at an arts festival before: a representative of all the thousands of artists who devoted their entire lives to a search for truth and beauty—and didn't find doodley-squat!" (37). Trout does, however, find himself mugged, bored to tears by people who give him rides, and finally almost involved in a fatal accident before he arrives in Indiana. Through his eyes, and through the accounts of dozens of sci-fi novels Trout has written, Vonnegut paints a bleak picture of a country that is "by far the richest and most powerful country on the planet. It had most of the food and minerals and machinery, and it disciplined other countries by threatening to shoot big rockets at them or to drop things on them from airplanes" (12).

While Trout moves across half the country, Dwayne Hoover moves in a smaller orbit around Midland City. A highly successful Pontiac dealer who seems to own half of the businesses in town, Hoover is nevertheless a desperately unhappy man. If Trout represents the frustrations in Vonnegut's professional life, Hoover embodies those of his personal life. The chief parallels are the suicides of a close relative (Vonnegut's mother and Hoover's wife, Celia, who killed herself by swallowing Drano) and the fear of insanity. Like his creator Hoover finds himself at sea after losing his wife of many years, and he careens about searching for some meaning behind all his suffering. Early in the novel he puts a pistol barrel in his mouth and nearly pulls the trigger. He settles at the last moment for shooting up his bathroom. The whole novel suggests that the violence endemic in American culture is this sort of death wish turned outward. And what is most disturbing is that these suicidal impulses come not from any grand philosophical stance but simply from bad chemistry. Vonnegut writes that "Dwayne's incipient insanity was mainly a matter of chemicals, of course. Dwayne

Hoover's body was manufacturing certain chemicals which unbalanced his mind" (13–14).

Vonnegut brings the two foci of his book—Trout and Hoover—together through yet another of Trout's sci-fi books. As an example of his work, from which he plans to read at the Arts Festival, Trout brings a copy of *Now It Can Be Told*. Its premise is that

Life was an experiment by the Creator of the Universe, Who wanted to test a new sort of creature He was think-ing of introducing into the Universe. It was a creature with the ability to make up its own mind. All the other creatures were fully programmed robots.

The book was in the form of a long letter from the Creator of the Universe to the experimental creature. The Creator congratulated the creature and apologized for all the discomfort he had endured" (178).

When Hoover reads the book after Trout gives it to him at the Holiday Inn lounge, he takes it as the truth and as an excuse to go on a rampage, since those he attacks are robots anyway. Although he doesn't kill anyone, it isn't for lack of trying: he breaks his mistress's ribs, smashes his son's face into his piano keyboard, and bites off the tip of one of Trout's fingers. The police finally subdue him and take him away in a straitjacket. The lawsuits resulting from this rampage eventually leave him a penniless bum on Midland City's skid row.

Despite this grim exit by Hoover, Vonnegut does not stop with the idea that human beings are programmed by the chemistry of their brains to act as they do. Seeing what effect his book had on Hoover, Trout realizes "that even *he* could bring evil into the world—in the form of bad ideas. And, after Dwayne was carted off to a lunatic asylum in a canvas camisole, Trout became a fanatic on the importance of ideas as causes and cures for diseases" (15). Vonnegut adds weight to his conclusion by having Trout win the Nobel Prize—for medicine—shortly before his death in 1981. When he enters the novel himself, Vonnegut likewise agrees that ideas matter, not just chemicals. He proclaims that "this was the reason Americans shot each other so often: It was a convenient literary device for ending short stories and books" (214–15). Hoping to correct the influence of the falsifying ideas in conventional stories, Vonnegut

resolved to shun storytelling. I would write about life. Every person would be exactly as important as any other. All facts would also be given equal weightiness. Nothing would be left out. Let others bring order to chaos. I would bring chaos to order, instead, which I think I have done.

If all writers would do that then perhaps citizens not in the literary trades will understand that there is no order in the world around us, that we must adapt ourselves to the requirements of chaos instead (215).

But the human mind can never be satisfied with either the certainty of philosophical determinism or the uncertainty of chaos. So at what Vonnegut calls "the spiritual climax of this book" he has an artist deliver an unexpectedly optimistic endorsement of the uniqueness of every individual—of a quality of sovereignty and will that gives dignity to human existence. Vonnegut confesses that because of his difficult times "I had come to the conclusion that there was nothing sacred about myself or about any human being, that we were all machines, doomed to collide and collide and collide" (224–25). But when an Abstract Expressionist painter of dubious merit named Rabo Karabekian delivers his defense of his art in the Holiday Inn lounge, Vonnegut is transformed. As he writes, "I did not expect Rabo Karabekian to rescue me. I had created him, and he was in my opinion a vain and weak and trashy man, no artist at all. But it is Rabo Karabekian who made me the serene Earthling which I am this day" (225). What Rabo says is that his seemingly simple painting, a single vertical stripe of orange on a dark field—a painting reviled by the uneducated Indiana bar crowd—is actually

a picture of the awareness of every animal. It is the immaterial core of every animal—the 'I am' to which all messages are sent. It is all that is alive in any of us—in a mouse, in a deer, in a cocktail waitress. It is unwavering and pure, no matter what preposterous adventure may befall us (226).

SLAPSTICK

Thus Vonnegut the atheist, the skeptical scientist, ends up affirming in yet another of his seemingly bleak books what idealists like Plato, the writers of the Gospels, and the author of *The Divine Comedy* have through the centuries all affirmed: Human beings have souls. Perhaps this is why Vonnegut chose as his epigraph a passage from the Book of Job that speaks of persisting in faith through difficult times: "When he hath tried me, I shall come forth as gold."

Slapstick

Published three years after *Breakfast of Champions*, *Slapstick* (1976) proved that the signs of exhaustion and lack of a clear direction in Vonnegut's early 1970s work were all too real. *Breakfast of Champions* had contained flashes of the brilliance Vonnegut displayed in his 1960s novels; *Slapstick* was an embarrassment. Shortly after its publication Vonnegut admitted that

Slapstick may be a very bad book. I am perfectly willing to believe that. Everybody else writes lousy books, so why shouldn't I? What was unusual about the reviews was that they wanted people to admit now that I had never been any good. The reviewer for the Sunday [*New York*] *Times* actually asked critics who had praised me in the past to now admit in public how wrong they'd been. . . . All of a sudden, critics wanted me squashed like a bug.[11]

Actually, some critics were unjustifiably positive about *Slapstick*, perhaps carrying over their enthusiasm for the Vonnegut of *Slaughterhouse-Five* to this novel; but those who looked at the book on its own terms saw little to praise. Vonnegut had to agree when he awarded grades to his work: he gave *Slaughterhouse-Five* an A-plus, *Breakfast of Champions* a C, and *Slapstick* a D.[12]

The novel begins with Vonnegut speaking directly to the reader, as he had in his previous two books. In *Slapstick*, however, he switches to a fictional first-person persona for the rest of the novel, with the exception of an epilogue in yet another point of view, the third person. Vonnegut's metafictional experiments with point of view in *Breakfast of Champions* had been controlled, consistently interesting, and thematically apt; here the three different ones seem the result of indecision. Of these points of view the prologue is the most successful, especially for what it reveals about the autobiographical sources of Vonnegut's artistry. Its first sentence reads: "This is the closest I will ever come to writing an autobiography." The next twenty-five pages or so do for Vonnegut's family life what *Slaughterhouse-Five* had done for his experience at Dresden: reveal how an early sense of loss and sorrow underlies his vision of a contemporary world in decline.

The chief sorrow revealed in the prologue was the death at age forty-one of Vonnegut's beloved sister Alice in 1958. The more immediate one was the death in 1975 of Vonnegut's Uncle Alex. Vonnegut and his brother Bernard boarded a plane and flew to Indianapolis for the funeral, and thought along the way of both their dead sister and the dispersal of the remaining children from their ancestral home. Vonnegut writes that he imagined the whole plot of *Slapstick* while on the flight. Considering the circumstances, it is not surprising that the novel concerns "desolated cities and spiritual cannibalism and incest and loneliness and lovelessness and death, and so on. It depicts myself and my beautiful sister as monsters, and so on. This is only natural, since I dreamed it on the way to a funeral."[13]

Nearing her death, Alice had remarked to Vonnegut that her situation was "slapstick"—so absurd and painful as to be almost comic. Vonnegut took the remark as the title of his novel, because like his sister's death it is "grotesque, situational poetry—like the slapstick film comedies" (1). Life is like a slapstick movie because, Vonnegut explains, "there are all these tests of my limited agility and intelligence. They go on and on." But in the world of slapstick—epitomized by the comedy of Laurel and Hardy, to whom the novel is dedicated—"the fundamental joke . . . was that they did their best with every test. They never failed to bargain in good faith with their destinies, and were screamingly adorable and funny on that account" (1). Vonnegut's fate was to be born into a German-American family that first had to deny its European heritage when the Germans became the enemy in World War I, then see its family prospects wrecked by the Depression; then to experience the firebombing of Dresden; then to have his sister and brother-in-law die within two days and leave him with three of their sons to raise. A strange destiny indeed—but one with which Vonnegut has unquestionably bargained in good faith through his personal and fictional efforts to resist despair.

Slapstick's major section is a fictionalized first-person account of Vonnegut's psychic struggle to regain the lost innocence and security of his childhood. Rather than being direct autobiography, it is "about what life *feels* like to me" (1). Vonnegut adopts the persona of Dr. Wilbur Daffodil-ll Swain, after confessing in the prologue that "I guess he is myself—experimenting with being old" (19). Alice becomes Wilbur's twin sister, Eliza Mellon Swain. The twins are "monsters," with six fingers on each hand and Neanderthaloid features: "massive brow-ridges, sloping foreheads, and steam-shovel jaws" (28). They are shockingly ugly to their parents, who send them away to a mansion surrounded by apple trees in Vermont. There Wilbur and Eliza live an Edenic life, attended to by servants, pretending to be retarded while actually developing into a sort of composite genius. Eliza is inductive in her thinking, while Wilbur is analytic; together they come up with all sorts of theories about gravity (they believe the ancient stone monuments were constructed when gravity was lighter than at present), the theory of evolution, and the necessity for creating artificial extended families. This latter idea becomes the central theme of the novel.

SLAPSTICK

Eliza and Wilbur lose their blissful existence as a "nation of two" when they overhear their mother telling their father, on one of their yearly visits to see them on their birthday, that she hates her grotesque children. In an attempt to make their parents feel better Eliza and Wilbur give up their pretense of being retarded and reveal their intelligence. The result, however, is that "intelligence and sensitivity in monstrous bodies like Elizas and mine merely made us more repulsive" (75). On the advice of a parodically evil child psychologist, Dr. Cordelia Swain Cordiner, the two are separated. Wilbur eventually becomes a pediatrician, Eliza a pushed-aside embarrassment who eventually gets a lawyer (Norman Mushari, who first appeared in *God Bless You, Mr. Rosewater*) and sues to get her part of the family inheritance.

This part of the narrative, as unlikely as it is, works fairly well as Vonnegut's exploration of the loss of childhood innocence. His two halves of the sexes joined in a presexual whole recalls such ancient myths as Plato's notion that the sexes were originally joined before being split by vindictive gods. Thus the melancholy searches of adults for ideal love simply reflect their attempts to regain that sense of wholeness they had in the past. As Vonnegut writes of Alice in his prologue, "She was the secret of whatever artistic unity I had ever achieved. She was the secret of my technique. Any creation which has any wholeness and harmoniousness, I suspect, was made by an artist or inventor with an audience of one in mind" (15).

As compensation for this lost sense of unity Vonnegut proposes the idea of creating artificial extended families. Wilbur eventually becomes President, and his major effort is to assign everyone in the country a new middle name—Chromium, Daffodil, Chipmunk. The new names create families who have directories and newsletters and reunions, and generally act like old-fashioned relatives—sometimes quarrelling but more often helping each other out. Reed wonders in his analysis of the novel just how serious Vonnegut is about this idea. He concludes that despite the fact that "the portrayal of the extended-family plan in *Slapstick* is hedged about with ironical—and farcical—undercutting . . . some reasonably serious defense of extended families survives."[14] When asked whether he had done any research into the possible validity of his scheme, Vonnegut admitted, "No. I'm afraid to. I might find out it wasn't true. It's a sunny little dream I have of a happier mankind. I couldn't survive my own pessimism if I didn't have some kind of sunny little dream."[15] Vonnegut believes that his dream of artificial extended families could render postmodern Americans, in the words of *Slapstick*'s subtitle, "Lonesome No More," the slogan that got Wilbur elected President.

Once Vonnegut memorializes his lost relationship with Alice through his prologue and the account of Wilbur and Eliza's early lives, and then states his theme of the need for artificial extended families, he has little left to say. Like *The Sirens of Titan* or *Galápagos*, *Slapstick* has a weak second half of ever more fantastic scenarios that ring increasingly false. Interspersed with Dr. Swain's account of his past with Eliza are scenes in the "present," when he is a hundred years old and living in the ruins of Manhattan—"the Island of Death." America has been decimated by the Albanian Flu and the Green Death—the former being caused by the ingestion of microscopic Chinese, who have found a way to shrink themselves, the latter by the inhalation of tiny invading Martians. Such flights of sci-fi fancy recall the excesses of *The Sirens of Titan* at its worst. New York and the rest of the nation have been wrecked by periodic onslaughts of heavy gravity, for which Vonnegut offers no real explanation. That the mysterious Chinese may be behind it is hinted at, but that whole motif is weakly conceived and does little to contribute to Vonnegut's themes of childhood bliss and extended families. The Chinese do serve to get Eliza to Mars late in the novel, where she dies in an avalanche.

A telling example of the exhaustion of Vonnegut's imagination in *Slapstick* is his tired refrain of "Hi ho." A sporty phrase ordinarily signaling a zest for life and a readiness for action, "Hi ho" becomes in this novel an ironic lament of weariness and passivity. "So it goes" in *Slaughterhouse-Five* had been extremely effective as a way to convey Vonnegut's complex attitudes toward the human condition; "And so on" was less so but not really bothersome in *Breakfast of Champions.* Vonnegut himself, however, seems annoyed with "Hi ho" in this book. He has Wilbur admit, "It is a thing I often say these days: 'Hi ho.' It is a kind of senile hiccup. I have lived too long. Hi ho" (23). After repeating the phrase past the point of annoyance, Wilbur says, "I swear: If I live to complete this autobiography, I will go through it again, and cross out all the 'Hi ho's.' Hi ho" (32). Unfortunately, Wilbur does not live long enough, so the reader is left with Vonnegut parodying himself.

Other flaws in *Slapstick* are impossible to ignore. Vonnegut makes much of the monstrous appearance of Wilbur and Eliza early in the novel but hardly mentions their looks later on. He offers no explanation for Wilbur's victory other than the effectiveness of his campaign slogan. Similarly the disintegration of America into petty states run by "the King of Michigan" or "the Duke of Oklahoma" is sketchily drawn and finds no effective satiric target. Published in the year of America's bicentennial celebration, with all its attendant boosterism and flag-waving, *Slapstick* is Vonnegut's alternative vision of a country coming apart under internal and external pressures. But without the unified apocalyptic vision of, say, *Cat's Cradle,* where Ice-9 is a metaphor for atomic weapons laying waste the planet, *Slapstick* lacks force as a critique of American moral failings. Vonnegut makes a halfhearted gesture at satirizing American religious fundamentalism in his passages on the Church of Jesus Christ the Kidnapped, but there is nothing here that comes close to his effective lampoons of religion in *Cat's Cradle* or *God Bless You, Mr. Rosewater.*

Finally, Vonnegut ends on the note of having Eliza talk with Wilbur from beyond the grave through a mechanical device called the Hooligan. It turns out that "the life after death is infinitely more tiresome than this one" (85). Yet Eliza urges Wilbur to join her as soon as possible, so they can be reunited at last. All this is recounted by the third-person narrator of the epilogue, who has already reported that "Dr. Swain died before he could write anymore" (229). In this narrative backtracking, the reader learns that Dr. Swain had returned from the Midwest, where the Hooligan was located, to Manhattan, where he expected the Green Death to finish him off. The novel ends with an account of how Dr. Swain's granddaughter, Melody, had walked all the way from the Midwest to find him, relying on relatives to help her along the journey. She had been raped, though, near Schenectady, and after her arrival had given birth to a stillborn child, which she and her new lover are burying under a pyramid during Dr. Swain's last days. She is pregnant again, so Dr. Swain will leave behind a great-grandson to try and survive in the postapocalyptic world.

Thus in *Slapstick* Vonnegut reaches back into his old bag of sci-fi tricks and pulls out everything he can grab—fluctuating gravity, microscopic Chinamen, invaders from Mars, communication with the spirit

UNDERSTANDING KURT VONNEGUT

world. Perhaps he does so with the vaudevillian's sense that the very predictability of his outlandish act—the pies in the face, the inevitable slips on the obvious banana peel—is part of the joke. But it seems more likely that after a decade of tremendously innovative fiction followed by the pressures of fame and personal troubles, Vonnegut had simply run out of the energy to fit his zanier ideas into a coherent whole. Apparently sensing the problem, he would abandon science fiction in his next two novels in favor of social/political realism and so initiate the second major phase of his career.

Notes

1. *Conversations with Kurt Vonnegut*, ed. William Rodney Allen (Jackson: University Press of Mississippi, 1988) 107. Hereafter *CKV*.

2. *Palm Sunday* (New York: Delacorte/Lawrence, 1981) 189.

3. *Palm Sunday* 304.

4. *Palm Sunday* 304.

5. *CKV* 108.

6. *CKV* 33.

7. *Breakfast of Champions* (New York: Delacorte/Lawrence, 1973) 4. Subsequent references are noted parenthetically.

8. *Vonnegut in America*, ed. Jerome Klinkowitz and Donald L. Lawler (New York: Delacorte/Lawrence, 1977) 154–55.

9. *CKV* 108.

10. Jerome Klinkowitz, *Kurt Vonnegut* (New York: Methuen, 1982) 71.

11. *CKV* 184.

12. *Palm Sunday* 312.
13. *Slapstick* (New York: Delacorte/Lawrence, 1976) 18–19. Subsequent references are noted parenthetically.
14. *Vonnegut in America* 176–77.
15. *CKV* 80.

CHAPTER SIX

Jailbird; Deadeye Dick

F. Scott Fitzgerald remarked that "American lives have no second acts." He meant that our youth-oriented culture tends to produce careers of great early promise that often fail to live up to their beginnings. Fitzgerald's own life, as he openly confessed, fit this pattern—a steep slide from early success as a writer into alcoholism, lack of productivity, and an early death. In the 1970s Vonnegut's career seemed to be going the way of Fitzgerald's. Drinking, divorce, and depression had taken their toll on him, and his tired rehashing of his old science fiction tricks in *Slapstick* looked like signs of an irreversible decline. But the appearance of *Jailbird* in 1979 marked the surprising resurgence of Vonnegut's career—a new vigor in his writing that can only be called a second major phase when one considers the cumulative effect of his four most recent novels. Vonnegut, who described himself as a flower that had bloomed when he published *Slaughterhouse-Five*, had withered for a decade only to blossom again in the 1980s.

124

Jailbird

The most striking thing about this latest phase of his work, with the exception of *Galápagos*, is Vonnegut's abandonment of science fiction in favor of social realism. The first words of the autobiographical prologue of *Jailbird* are: "Yes—Kilgore Trout is back again." But this pronouncement is misleading to the reader expecting a book like *The Sirens of Titan* to follow. Trout is not back as the "real" character he was in *God Bless You, Mr. Rosewater, Slaughterhouse-Five*, and *Breakfast of Champions*, but rather merely as the sci-fi pen name of one of the protagonist's fellow inmates at a federal prison. While many of *Jailbird*'s events are highly fanciful and unlikely, they do not involve time travel, changes in gravitational force, or visits from extraterrestrials. In terms of the imaginative space it occupies, the world of the novel is the mundane one the average person inhabits. Only in *Mother Night* had Vonnegut previously attempted such a book devoid of his trademark sci-fi special effects. Perhaps realizing after the disastrous reception of *Slapstick* that he had exhausted the possibilities of fantasy writing, he turned once again to the description of ordinary human experience.

The result was Vonnegut's most intensely felt novel since *Slaughterhouse-Five*. Despite its being the autobiography of an aging, guilt-ridden, nearly exhausted man, *Jailbird* is filled with vivid, memorable scenes and characters. Its chief subject is Vonnegut's moral outrage at the social injustice in America in the twentieth century. Its most immediate historical reference is to the Watergate scandal of the early 1970s—the Republican break-in at the Democratic campaign headquarters and its attempted cover-up that led to the only resignation of a President of the United States in our history. Richard Nixon appears in the book, as do many real-life people and events. Interwoven with them are Vonnegut's fictional characters, who serve to make the historical events come alive by being eyewitnesses to and participants in them. Just as the imagined characters balance the actual historical people, the account of an episode of what might be called invented history—the massacre of striking workers at a factory—balances the real events of Watergate. The result is an intriguing blend of fact and fiction, one characteristic of several notable American novels of the 1970s.

So vivid is the account in the prologue of the massacre of striking workers at the Cuyahoga Bridge and Iron Company in Cleveland in 1894 that some readers of *Jailbird* have taken it for an actual event. But as Vonnegut writes, before recounting it, the massacre "is an invention, a mosaic composed of bits taken from tales of many such riots in not such olden times."[1] Thus the novel reads like a history of the United States from the labor unrest of the turn of the century to the aftermath of Watergate. In between lie wars, economic booms and busts, witch-hunts for communists, the sexual revolution. History is so vital to the novel that its protagonist,

JAILBIRD

Walter F. Starbuck, proclaims that "years as well as people are characters in this book, which is the story of my
life so far" (1).

As *Jailbird* opens, Vonnegut's protagonist is about
to be released from federal prison in Atlanta, Georgia,
where he has been serving time for his part in the Watergate affair. Rather than being at the center of the
conspiracy, Starbuck fell into it by accident, when some
of Nixon's men chose his basement office in the White
House in which to hide a million dollars in illegal campaign contributions. He had gone to prison for refusing
to name the men who hid the cash. The rest of the novel
unfolds the irony that a man who had been a communist in his youth would end up working for a Republican president as his Advisor to Youth Affairs and
lumped in the public's mind with the right-wing zealots
of the Watergate hearings and trials.

At the age of sixty-six Starbuck seems ill prepared
to start a new life on the outside after two years in Jail.
He sits staring straight ahead on his cot, waiting for a
guard to usher him out who looks just like Jimmy Carter
and who is in fact the new President's third cousin,
realizing that "there would be no one to greet me at the
gate. Nowhere in the world was there anyone who had
a forgiving hug for me—or a free meal or a bed for a
night or two" (2). He is like Rip Van Winkle waking up
after a long sleep to find himself in an alien world. And
as Washington Irving had done in his story, Vonnegut
uses his protagonist's sense of being out of his time to

UNDERSTANDING KURT VONNEGUT

comment on contemporary culture—in this case to satirize current crazes like jogging and born-again Christianity of the Charles Coleson variety. But the first half
of *Jailbird* focuses on Starbuck's looking backward over
the remarkable life that brought him to his prison cell
in Georgia.

As Jerome Klinkowitz writes, "*Jailbird* tries to re-
construct practically everything [in American life] from
capitalism to Christianity. . . . [It] tinkers with a bit of
economics here and a bit of religion there until a sub-
stantially new vision of American life emerges."[2] Most
simply put, the "new vision" Vonnegut wants to present is one countering the prevailing American Cold
War doctrine that most of the evil in the twentieth century (with the notable exception of the Nazis) was
caused by left-wingers or outright communists. Recall-
ing the repression of labor movements, the miscarriage
of justice in the infamous Sacco and Vanzetti trial, and
the fanatical persecution of anyone with left-wing ties
in the McCarthy era, Vonnegut shows through Starbuck's account of his life that it is impossible for the
right wing in America to claim the high moral ground.
Moreover, as he suffers through the harangues of born-
again hard-liners like Emil Larkin, whose "witnessing"
consists mostly of insults about Starbuck's left-wing
past, Starbuck points out the obvious parallels between
the communist ideal and Christianity. In the former, all
men and women cooperate, as opposed to acting self-
ishly as they are encouraged to do by capitalism. As he

wonders early in his story, thinking of his days in the party in the 1930s,

What could be so repulsive after all, during the Great Depression, especially, . . . in a young man's belief that each person could work as well as he or she was able, and should be rewarded, sick or well, young or old, brave or frightened, talented or imbecilic, according to his or her simple needs? How could anyone treat me as a person with a diseased mind if I thought that war need never come again—if only common people every-where would take control of the planet's wealth, dis-band their national armies, and forget their national boundaries; if only they would think of themselves ever after as brothers and sisters, yes, and as mothers and fathers, too, and children of all common people—every-where. . . .
    And even now, at the rueful age of sixty-six, I find my knees still turn to water when I encounter anyone who still considers it a possibility that there will one day be one big happy and peaceful family on Earth—the Family of Man (13–14).

Jailbird is largely the story of the subverters of that ideal, including Starbuck himself; yet it contains portraits of a few brave souls heroic enough to maintain it despite all odds.
    Watergate showed that the subverters of the ideal of the Family of Man—not to mention the Constitution of the United States—could be found in the White

House; the story of the trial and execution of Sacco and Vanzetti shows that they may also sit on the judicial bench; and finally, the invented story of the Cuyahoga massacre suggests that they can be found heading America's corporations. Vonnegut explained in an interview that he wrote the section on the Cuyahoga massacre because "the history of the labor movement holds a special interest for me."[3] In its early days that story was one, almost exclusively, of defeat, and Vonnegut reflects that in his story of the brutal repression of unarmed workers by the McCones, the owners of the company. Daniel McCone had fired his workers when they refused to take a 10 percent cut in pay and replaced them with men desperate enough to work at that rate. Evicted from their homes, they staged a demonstration in front of the factory gates on Christmas morning. When they refused to disperse after being read the riot act, National Guard troops began to move on them, which resulted in panic and the killing of fourteen people by sharpshooters. The real inspiration for the Cuyahoga episode was not the labor riots of the turn of the century but the fatal shooting of four students by National Guard troops on the campus of Kent State University in 1970. Vonnegut revealed the connection when he complained about "our enduring delusion about the National Guard, . . . the hallucination that any American handed a rifle was thereby transformed into a soldier. The last time that theory was tested was at Kent State. . . . It's hard for me to imagine any kind of sane

JAILBIRD

government which would conclude people like that had any business holding loaded rifles."[4] Vonnegut tells the Cuyahoga story economically, with an amazingly sharp eye for details: it is one of the best examples in his fiction of his ability to convey his deepest political convictions through vivid fiction.

This is most clearly demonstrated in Vonnegut's retelling of the story of Sacco and Vanzetti, which in many ways is the heart of the novel. They were executed in 1927, and now Starbuck finds almost no one under thirty has even heard their names. As he muses, "When I was a young man, I expected the story of Sacco and Vanzetti to be retold as often and as movingly, to be as irresistible, as the story of Jesus Christ some day" (171). But such is not the case, so Starbuck proceeds to present the facts of one of the worst miscarriages of justice in our history. Italian immigrants who came to the United States in 1908, Sacco and Vanzetti were arrested for trying to organize strikes and were blacklisted by employers hoping to starve out "troublemakers." In 1920 they were arrested and charged with the murder of two payroll guards in a holdup. The evidence against them was virtually nonexistent, but the judge of the case said of Vanzetti that "although he may not have actually committed the crime attributed to him [he] is nevertheless morally culpable, because he is the enemy of our existing institutions" (177–78). Despite world outcry after their conviction and pleas for a new trial by such figures as George Bernard Shaw, Albert Einstein, and H. G. Wells, Sacco and Vanzetti were executed, even though another man had confessed to and been put to death for their alleged crimes. For Vonnegut their story is a tragic reminder of what can happen when due process of law is swept aside so that individuals can be persecuted for their political beliefs. "Although it's such a fascinating story, people really don't like to hear it retold," he has said. "Maybe if it does get retold five more times during the next ten years it may become a little more central to our culture. Because, damn it, the story is so shaking and moving—one of the most impressive I know."[5]

Charles Berryman writes that "Vonnegut agrees with several of his critics who feel that *Jailbird* is a better book than its predecessor. . . . Perhaps the difference has to do with the power of history in fiction. The detailed accounts of massacre and execution in *Jailbird* raise questions of public guilt and morality that cannot be invoked by the bizarre events of the earlier novel."[6] The "power of history" is an apt phrase to explain the success of Vonnegut's recent fiction; moreover, his examples from history in *Jailbird* are not exclusively negative, but also include a small group of heroes who keep alive the dream of the Family of Man. The most selfless of these idealists is the real-life labor organizer Powers Hapgood, whom Vonnegut met once at a lunch with his father in 1945. In contrast to his father, who had been so dispirited by losing his work as an architect in the Depression that he was "in full retreat from life,"

Hapgood was a Harvard graduate who turned away from his life of privilege in order to help the downtrodden laborers battered by the economic turmoil of the times. He was "still full of ideas of how victory might yet be snatched from the jaws of defeat"—unlike Kurt Vonnegut, Sr., who had long since given up the fight. Thinking of such men as Hapgood, Vonnegut records in his prologue that he had realized "if I am going to go on living, . . . I had better follow them" (xiii).

In *Jailbird* Hapgood becomes Kenneth Whistler, who resembles him in most respects. Starbuck and his girlfriend, Mary Kathleen O'Looney, had heard Whistler speak at a labor rally at Harvard during the Depression and had been swept away by his passion, eloquence, and moral authority. After the speech, when Mary Kathleen had whispered in Starbuck's ear, "You're going to be just like him, Walter," Starbuck had replied, "I'll try." But even as he says that, he realizes "I had no intention of trying" (171). *Jailbird* is the story of a man who often lacks the moral courage to live up to his ideals—who knows what is right but fears the consequences of doing it. Years after hearing Whistler, Starbuck confesses that "I was never a serious man. I have been in a lot of trouble over the years, but that was all accidental. Never have I risked my life, or even my comfort, in the service of mankind. Shame on me" (171). Yet unlike so many of his fellow Americans, Starbuck at least realizes his moral failings and feels guilty about them. The reader finds it impossible to disagree when Mary Kathleen runs into Starbuck on a street corner in New York City just after he is released and exclaims, "Thank God you're still alive! Thank God there's somebody still alive who cares what happens to this country. I thought maybe I was the last one" (157).

Starbuck clearly does care, even though he is reviled by those who remember him either as a communist or as a right-wing fanatic in league with Nixon. Starbuck's chief sin, which torments his conscience for nearly three decades, was his testimony before a 1949 Congressional hearing that his friend Lewland Clewes had been a member of the Communist Party back in the 1930s. Despite simply having told the truth, Starbuck was viewed as a traitor by his fellow workers in the federal bureaucracy, and soon found himself out of a job. While he eventually made it back into government service, his refusal to name the "bag men" for Nixon's illegal million dollars found in his office led to his imprisonment and second period of infamy. Torn between his impulse to tell the truth and to be loyal to morally suspect colleagues and organizations, Starbuck is punished for doing both, thus showing the ambiguity of ethical decisions in the complexities of twentieth-century politics.

But as always in Vonnegut's fiction simple human decency offers a way out of the confusion. Just before he runs into Mary Kathleen on his first day back in New York, Starbuck's self-esteem hits rock bottom as he tries to find a place to eat and rest:

JAILBIRD

I believed that I was the ugliest, dirtiest little old bum in Manhattan. If I went into the coffee shop, everybody would be nauseated. They would throw me out and tell me to go to the Bowery, where I belonged.

But I somehow found the courage to go in anyway—and imagine my surprise! It was as though I had died and gone to heaven! A waitress said to me, "Honeybunch, you sit right down, and I'll bring you your coffee right away." I hadn't said anything to her.

So I did sit down, and everywhere I looked I saw customers of every description being received with love (123).

The whole novel turns on this hopeful incident, for a few minutes later Starbuck has his rendezvous with Mary Kathleen O'Looney, his old girlfriend. Of this unlikely meeting, Vonnegut remarked that "an author gets to a point where he needs a couple of coincidences to keep the story moving, and he doesn't dare pause for thirty pages to contrive an elaborate sequence of believable events in order to get a few characters together. So, he takes a deep breath and treats himself to a coincidence."[7]

Early in his reminiscence Starbuck says he has "loved only four women in my life—my mother, my late wife, a woman to whom I was once affianced, and one other" (9). Sarah was the fiancée, Mary Kathleen O'Looney the "one other." In contrast to the power-hungry men in *Jailbird* these women, though radically different from each other, offer a gentler alternative to masculine ruthlessness and duplicity. Starbuck calls them "more virtuous, braver about life, and closer to the secrets of the universe than I could ever be" (9). Starbuck's wife, Ruth, had survived the concentration camps that killed her parents and had amazed her husband with her knowledge and ability to love after what she had been through. Sarah, an heiress fallen on hard times, had found refuge in humor, swapping jokes with Starbuck over the years even after they broke up. But Mary Kathleen's story is the most amazing of all. The second half of *Jailbird* is more akin to *God Bless You, Mr. Rosewater* than to any other Vonnegut novel, for it too features a wealthy person's attempt to return the riches he or she possesses to the common people.

Mary Kathleen O'Looney had married well after being jilted by Starbuck, had become Mrs. Jack Graham, a multimillionaire's wife. After his death she heads the RAMJAC Corporation, which Starbuck describes as controlling nearly one-fifth of the wealth of the United States. In an obvious reference to the strange career of Howard Hughes, another reclusive millionaire, Vonnegut has her run her vast empire in hiding, disguised as bag lady to avoid kidnappers and con artists. Starbuck's reunion with Mary Kathleen and their subsequent adventures—they round up all the people who have been nice to Starbuck and give them important jobs in RAMJAC—is somewhat at odds in its whimsy with the tough realism of the book's first half. But Vonnegut avoids sentimentality by having their scheme fail when the lawyers and the government take over nearly all the wealth of RAMJAC before it gets to the people. Mary Kathleen dies after being hit by a cab, but not before forgiving Starbuck's weaknesses by saying, "At least you tried to believe what the people with hearts believed—so you were a good man just the same" (220).

Berryman claims of Starbuck that he is "so inhibited by guilt and fear that he is incapable of any genuine passion," and that this lack "leaves the reader feeling indifferent to the fate of the character."[8] But surely this is off the mark. Starbuck *is* inhibited by guilt and fear, but he is anything but passionless; his flat affect is simply a defense against the chaotic emotions boiling inside him. The feeling underlying his accounts of Kenneth Whistler's idealistic life and the tragedy of Sacco and Vanzetti is some of the most profound in Vonnegut's fiction. At the novel's end, on his way back to prison for having hidden Mary Kathleen's will from the authorities so as to keep the lawyers at bay for a little while longer, Starbuck listens to a tape recording of his testimony to the Congressional committee in 1949 that had led to Clewes's downfall. On it he hears a remark that epitomizes his enduring idealism. When then Congressman Richard Nixon had asked him why he "had been so ungrateful to the American economic system" as to become a communist, Starbuck had used Whistler's reply on a similar occasion: "Why? The Sermon on the Mount, sir" (240–41). Starbuck's passionate hope in *Jailbird* is that someday the meek may indeed inherit the earth.

Deadeye Dick

In some respects *Deadeye Dick* (1982) seems like a rewrite of *Jailbird,* for both novels are first-person accounts told by melancholy older men who committed crimes that have cast a shadow over their whole lives. Both books are intricately tied up with historical events in America in this century, and both present Vonnegut's alternative vision of the meaning of that history. *Jailbird* is a warning that every generation in America has seen the ideals of the Constitution threatened—by the antilabor hysteria epitomized by the Sacco and Vanzetti executions in the 1920s, by the anticommunist fervor of the McCarthy era, even by the President and his men in Watergate in the early 1970s. Likewise *Deadeye Dick* is highly political, being at least implicitly Vonnegut's plea for gun control and putting an end to the arms race. Both novels are successful in dramatizing Vonnegut's interpretation of our history because they intertwine those political concerns with fascinating, inventive accounts of the protagonist's experience. While Vonnegut warns the reader that *Deadeye Dick* "is fiction, not history,"[9] he could easily have said that it is both.

Vonnegut's by-now standard autobiographical introduction is short but important in this novel. In his

preface he adopts his old strategy of intentionally dif-
fusing suspense by announcing that "I will explain the
main symbols in this book" (xii). The last two and presumably the most important are that "the neutered
pharmacist who tells the tale is my declining sexuality.
The crime he committed in childhood is all the bad
things I have done" (xiii). Rudy Waltz is the protagonist;
his childhood crime was accidentally killing a pregnant
woman when he fired a rifle out of a window of his
house. By openly admitting autobiographical impulses
behind his creation of Rudy Waltz, Vonnegut almost
demands that the reader speculate about "all the bad
things" that could have caused him such guilt. Once
such speculation begins, numerous parallels quickly
emerge between the characters in the book and their
creator.

On one level *Deadeye Dick* is Vonnegut's most intensely personal fictional exploration of his unhappy
relationship with his parents. Rudy's father, Otto, is a
psychological though not factual portrait of Vonnegut's
father. Both men had German backgrounds they had to
suppress when World War II began, both were artistic
(though Otto was so only in a bogus way), and both
were effectively crushed in spirit by early middle age
and so could not show much in the way of paternal
warmth to their sons. Kurt Vonnegut, Sr., was crushed
by losing his work as an architect during the Depression, Otto by being beaten up by the police and going
to jail for allowing Rudy access to his gun collection at

such a young age. The deeply shamed Rudy admits that despite Otto's artistic pretensions, despite his posing as a deeply learned world traveler, in the moment of their crisis his father turned out to be "collapsible" (95). Moreover, Rudy's mother resembles Vonnegut's mother even more than Otto resembles his father. Both women were born into rich families, and both proved absolutely ineffectual as mothers and so allowed servants to raise their children. When economic reversals came to them, each simply gave up. As Rudy writes in a painfully moving passage, just after he returns home from his humiliation at the police station, Mrs. Waltz failed even to touch him in consolation, causing him to conclude that as a mother "she was purely ornamental. . . . She wasn't wicked. She simply wasn't useful" (93).

Why should having ineffectual parents be a cause for Vonnegut himself to feel such shame? In a revealing essay entitled "Embarrassment" he confesses that "a bad dream I have dreamed for as long as I can remember may hold a clue. In that dream, I know that I have murdered an old woman a long time ago." He goes on to speculate, "Could that woman be my mother? I asked a psychiatrist that. She said the woman might not even be a woman. She could be a man."[10] It seems reasonable to conclude that Vonnegut's dream about killing an older person may reflect anger at both his parents and that his sense of shame in part proceeds from that source. Berryman has pointed out that "Vonnegut dreams repeatedly about the murder of a woman, and all of his recent novels have important female characters who come to tragic ends," and he goes on to conclude that "the prevalence of this psychological drama may also contribute to the success of *Jailbird* and *Deadeye Dick*, while its absence may help to explain the weakness of *Breakfast of Champions* and *Slapstick*."[11]

Vonnegut's embarrassment also proceeds from the failure of his first marriage, an embarrassment reflected in Rudy's sense of being "neutered." While he never marries, in fact suspects himself of being a homosexual, Rudy strongly reflects Vonnegut's sense of being emotionally used up for a long time after he and Jane divorced. All through *Palm Sunday* Vonnegut gives painful accounts of his loneliness, depression, and sense of having lived past his period of usefulness in the 1970s. He has Rudy put it: "We all see our lives as stories. . . . If a person survives an ordinary span of sixty years or more, there is every chance that his or her life as a shapely story has ended, and all that remains to be experienced is epilogue. Life is not over, but the story is" (208). But while Rudy concludes that his life is essentially over as a story after the funeral of Celia Hoover— over because she had been the only person he had loved "at least a little bit" (176) since withdrawing emotionally after the shooting incident—Vonnegut himself had managed to recover from his period of despondency. His marriage to Jill Krementz in 1979 and his publication of *Jailbird* in that same year mark a decidedly happier and more productive chapter in his life. Ironically, he used the materials of his sense of failure and guilt to create some of the best work of his career.

Finally, *Deadeye Dick* deals with Vonnegut's guilt over his most embarrassing artistic failure. Even worse than the negative critical response to *Slapstick* were his feelings of incompetence arising out of the Broadway production of his play, *Happy Birthday, Wanda Jane* (1970). As he reveals in *Palm Sunday*, Vonnegut tried several endings for his rather wooden plea for peace featuring a parody of Hemingway as the main character, revising the play right up until opening night—which he spent in a drunken stupor to ease his embarrassment. He tries to exorcise the ghost of this ten-year-old failure by retelling it in *Deadeye Dick*. Rudy wins a contest for drama, the prize for which is having his play produced in New York. Rudy's entry, *Katmandu*, has all the half-baked philosophical yearning and dramatic ineptitude of its real-life model. Not surprisingly, "the play was a catastrophe" (129), and the experience, rather than being a triumphant coming-out, only drives Rudy further back into his emotional shell.

Deadeye Dick looks backward into the 1970s not only to Vonnegut's play but to his fiction, for it contains much of the material of *Breakfast of Champions* in a more realistic form. Celia Hoover threatens to take over the second half of the book, much as Mary Kathleen O'Looney does the second half of *Jailbird*. Even more than reflecting Vonnegut's habit of reintroducing char-

DEADEYE DICK

acters from earlier books into later ones, his elaboration on Celia's story seems to indicate his desire to get right a story he had failed to tell satisfactorily the first time. In *Deadeye Dick* she is a more fully developed character than in *Breakfast of Champions,* even through the causes of her despair and eventual suicide ultimately remain a mystery. She never fits perfectly into the structure of the novel, but Vonnegut simply cannot seem to let her go. Tellingly, the novel's epigraph is from Shakespeare by way of Otto Waltz: "Who is Celia? What is she? That all our swains commend her?" The amount of space Vonnegut gives to her characterization and the weight he gives to her funeral scene—at which all the major characters assemble and Rudy is finally granted forgiveness by the minister for his crime—suggest how much he wants to get her right. At the end of the novel a Haitian raises the spirit of one of Midland City's residents from the dead: *Deadeye Dick* is in part Vonnegut's attempt to do the same for Celia Hoover.

Deadeye Dick is basically realistic, but it is metafictional at the same time. Vonnegut calls attention to the artificiality of his discourse not only by using characters from earlier novels but by rendering crucial episodes in *Deadeye Dick* in the form of plays. As Rudy explains, "I have this trick for dealing with my worst memories. I insist that they are plays. The characters are actors. Their speeches and movements are stylized, arch" (83–84). Four times in the novel Vonnegut resorts to this device, all at moments of great embarrassment for

Rudy. The effect is richly paradoxical, for while the metafictional play-within-the-play aspect of these passages calls attention to the unreality of the characters and situations, Rudy's desperate need to distance himself from those situations by turning them into art comes through so strongly that he seems all the more real.

These four plays within the larger narrative mark the crucial moments in Rudy's life as well as the central themes of the novel. The first comes when Rudy finds himself being humiliated and physically abused by the police just after he accidentally shot the pregnant woman. This trauma of course affects him for life and explains most of his later behavior. Thematically the episode serves two purposes: to show how easily the passion for revenge can lead to the subversion of the accused's civil liberties, and to suggest that there are simply too many guns and gun nuts in America. When the police invite the husband of the dead woman to beat Rudy, however, he refuses, proving that it is possible to resist the very human tendency to join a lynch mob. This decent man's response to the tragedy of his wife's death is to write an editorial in his newspaper that echoes Vonnegut's own feelings on the subject: "My wife has been killed by a machine which should never have come into the hands of any human being. . . . We cannot get rid of mankind's fleetingly wicked wishes. We can get rid of the machines that make them come true. I give you one holy word: DISARM" (87).

DEADEYE DICK

Rudy's second "play" comes right before the disaster of the opening of his real play on Broadway. In it he overhears his brother's fight with his wife, which culminates in her charge that Rudy "would enjoy being a woman" (137), that he is "a circus freak" (139), and that he has terrible body odor and needs a bath. All this of course ensures Rudy's abject humiliation when the play fails, and shows him for good that he should never again try to come out of his shell. In the third "play" Celia Hoover comes into Rudy's pharmacy years later to express her admiration for Rudy and *Katmandu*, in which she had acted in a local production. Yet this once-beautiful woman has been ravaged by amphetamine addiction, and when Rudy misinterprets her praise as an attempt to get drugs she turns violent and wrecks the place before running out into the night.

The final "play" occurs at Celia's funeral, when Felix confesses to her husband that he too loved Celia. Rather than getting angry, Dwayne admits that he was unable to help his wife and tells Felix, "You should have married her, not me" (206). Rudy, the "neutered" pharmacist, merely looks on, doing what he can to distance himself from all the pain. Having lost his one chance for love with Celia, he now turns to a sort of marriage with his non-nurturing mother. She is alone after losing her husband in a blizzard that engulfed Midland City. Finally, *Deadeye Dick* offers the sober message that some emotional scars may simply be too deep to heal. Immaturity and bad luck combined to mark Rudy for life. Try as he might to recover through the power of art and love, he will always seem to the world the sick killer bearing the derisive nickname of Deadeye Dick.

As Vonnegut writes in the novel, lives are like stories, with main plots and epilogues. The book itself has an epilogue, one which, writ large, parallels Rudy's tragic life. In it Vonnegut harks back to his sci-fi past—and looks forward to the futuristic *Galápagos*—by having Midland City destroyed by a neutron bomb. This conclusion corresponds to Rudy's shooting of the pregnant woman, for it also depicts the dangers of having too many weapons around. Vonnegut may have chosen to end this book this way in order to provide a dramatic finale to Rudy's story—to end with a bang rather than with a whimper, to reverse T. S. Eliot's famous line. Further, always underlying his work is the apocalyptic experience of Dresden, the real-life model for his at-times seemingly overly pessimistic fictional world.

But more important than the technical demands of the novel or his experience in World War II in shaping the ending of *Deadeye Dick* is Vonnegut's outrage at the madness of the arms race, particularly as it was proceeding in the early 1980s. The newly developed neutron bomb seemed the final insult to humanity—a weapon designed by our government to kill people but leave most buildings intact. When Rudy and Felix return to their deserted city, they find that everything is exactly where it was when the bomb went off, "so that camera crews could document, without the least bit of fakery, the fundamental harmlessness of a neutron bomb" (229). Vonnegut stretches credulity by hinting that the explosion might not have been an accident but rather a plot by the government to subvert democracy and perhaps even bring back slavery. But his point is anything but an exaggeration: the United States government has lied to its citizens before, and may do so again. As Vonnegut said at an antinuclear rally in Washington on May 6, 1979: "We Americans have guided our destinies so clumsily, with all the world watching, that we must now protect ourselves against our own government and our own industries. Not to do so would be suicide."[12] In a 1980 interview he warned that "more weapons are manufactured every day and more arguments are gladly entered into and more enormous, dangerous lies are told, so there's no restraint. . . . We're totally warlike, and sooner or later something's going to go wrong."[13] By having Rudy Waltz fire the fatal shot from his father's gun, Vonnegut is reminding his readers that, given human nature, a nuclear missile may one day rise from its silo and begin the annihilation of humanity.

Notes

1. *Jailbird* (New York: Delacorte/Lawrence, 1979) xxi. Subsequent references are noted parenthetically.

2. Jerome Klinkowitz, *Kurt Vonnegut* (New York: Methuen, 1982) 79.

3. *Conversations with Kurt Vonnegut*, ed. William Rodney Allen (Jackson: University Press of Mississippi, 1988) 217. Hereafter *CKV*.

4. *CKV* 219.

5. *CKV* 217.

6. Charles Berryman, "After the Fall: Kurt Vonnegut," *Critique* 26 (1985) 97.

7. *CKV* 222.

8. Berryman 100.

9. *Deadeye Dick* (New York: Delacorte/Lawrence, 1982) xii. Subsequent references are noted parenthetically.

10. *Palm Sunday* (New York: Delacorte/Lawrence, 1981) 189–90.

11. Berryman 99, 101.

12. *Palm Sunday* 71.

13. *CKV* 239.

CHAPTER SEVEN

Galápagos; Bluebeard

Among Vonnegut's four most recent novels *Galápagos* stands out as an anomaly. *Jailbird, Deadeye Dick*, and *Bluebeard* are realistic fictions, dealing with contemporary characters in familiar settings, with no intrusions of supernatural events; *Galápagos,* on the other hand, is narrated by a ghost and covers a span of a million years of highly fanciful human history. But it would be a mistake to view the novel as simply a return to the science fiction excesses of *Slapstick* or *The Sirens of Titan*. While those earlier books had much to do with fantasy but little to do with hard science, *Galápagos* reflects Vonnegut's knowledge of the work of scientists like Carl Sagan and Stephen Jay Gould and often reads like a textbook in evolutionary biology. Excepting its supernatural narrator, it clearly belongs at the scientific, realistic pole of science fiction. After the almost claustrophobic explorations of the mind of a guilt-ridden protagonist in *Jailbird* and *Deadeye Dick,* Vonnegut apparently was ready to open up his perspective in a bold new experiment—a cerebral, at times chillingly impersonal contemplation of the possibility that humans may evolve away from higher intelligence and revert to a simpler animal existence.

The story line of *Galápagos* is simple: entrepreneurs in New York and South America have decided to cash in on the fascination of the general public with science in the 1980s by arranging the "Nature Cruise of the Century" to the Galápagos Islands. Such notables as Mick Jagger and Jackie Kennedy Onassis sign up for the trip aboard the luxury ship *Bahiá de Darwin*, but cancel their reservations when a worldwide financial crisis leads to food riots in Ecuador. Only a few passengers show up, including Mary Hepburn, a recently widowed schoolteacher, and James Wait, a gigolo who has married seventeen women in order to get their money before abandoning them. Others include a Japanese computer whiz and his pregnant wife, and an entrepreneur named Andrew MacIntosh, who plans to buy up half of Ecuador at bargain prices during the panic. When war breaks out between Peru and Ecuador, Captain Adolf von Kleist sets sail with Wait, Hepburn, and a few others, and eventually runs aground on the Galápagos Islands off the South American coast. There the group stays, becoming the only surviving members of the human race after a virus attacks the ovaries of all females everywhere else on the globe. By the time of the novel's "present," one million years from 1986, the human race has become a fur-covered group of fish-eating mammals with flippers rather than hands and a greatly diminished mental capacity. In *Galápagos*, Vonnegut's narrator writes that there is only one "real villain in my story: the oversize human brain."[1]

In an interview Vonnegut said that in *Galápagos* he could depict and even accept the loss of human emotional complexity made possible by our large brains for one simple reason: "Well, having seen where we're headed, I don't want to go that way anymore."[2] From his perspective the way human culture was headed in the early 1980s was particularly distressing. His radical solution in this novel of abandoning higher thought processes arose from several historical causes that greatly concerned Vonnegut. First, the worldwide financial panic in the book is an exaggeration of the deep recession that gripped the global economy in 1982. Unemployment was at its highest rate in America since the Depression—a fact that would have had special significance for a child of the Depression whose father was emotionally broken by it. Second, the concern over war breaking out, although a constant one in Vonnegut's work, was surely heightened by the war in the Falkland Islands between Britain and Argentina in 1982, and much more by the unprecedented arms buildup in America by the Reagan administration. Finally, the sexually related disease that destroys most of the human race in the novel reflects Americans' shock and fear at the discovery in the mid-1980s that millions of people around the world were infected with a new, incurable, sexually transmitted disease—AIDS. Arising out of this troubled climate, *Galápagos* is a somber, chilling book reflecting its author's pessimism about the chances for the survival of humanity. In it mankind does survive, but only by ceasing to be fully human.

The eerie impersonality of *Galápagos* is evident from the beginning. Unlike most of Vonnegut's novels it does not feature an autobiographical preface. These prefaces in the other books quickly establish a familiar relationship between author and reader, and often encourage the reader to identify Vonnegut with his protagonists. No such familiarity arises in *Galápagos*. The narrator of the novel turns out to be the dead son of Kilgore Trout, Vonnegut's old standby alter ego. Leon Trotsky Trout had worked on building the *Bahiá de Darwin* in Sweden, but had been decapitated when a sheet of steel fell on him in the drydock; he is present to record the events of the trip to the Galápagos because his ghost haunts the ship. Vonnegut explains that he came up with a ghost for a narrator because "I had the technical problem of point of view. The problem was, who's going to watch for a million years? A difficulty with writing novels is that the reader inevitably is going to ask, who's telling this? You wish he wouldn't, but he does. And you have to answer the question."[3] It is telling that the habit of first-person narration had become so ingrained in Vonnegut in his later books that he says he never even considered using the omniscient point of view in *Galápagos*. When one thinks of Vonnegut's recent fiction, the voices of his first-person narrators usually spring to

mind—particular people in sometimes extraordinary circumstances, like Walter Starbuck, Rudy Waltz, and the
memorable Rabo Karabekian of *Bluebeard*.

Unfortunately Leon Trout does not measure up to
Vonnegut's other recent protagonists either in terms of
fullness of development or integration into the larger
themes of the novel. Vonnegut seems unable to decide
whether to pursue Leon's story, a central event of
which was his participation in a massacre of civilians in
the Vietnam war, or simply to have him function as an
observer of the "Nature Cruise of the Century." The
climax of the former comes when Leon confronts the
spirit of his father, who urges him to give up his ghostly
existence on earth and enter the "blue tunnel" leading
to the afterlife. In Vonnegut's last word on Kilgore
Trout so far he makes his sci-fi hack the voice of despair
who must be rejected, for the dead father tells his dead
son that

the more you learn about people the more disgusted
you'll become. I would have thought that your being
sent by the wisest men in your country, supposedly, to
fight a nearly endless, thankless, horrifying, and, finally, pointless war, would have given you sufficient
insight into the nature of humanity to last you throughout all eternity! (254).

Leon considers entering the tunnel to join his father,
and listens to him recount the horrors of nuclear weap-

ons, pollution, and corrupt leadership, but he finally pulls back, deciding that "one reason, surely, that I found it hard to take another step in his direction was that I did not like him" (255). The despairing Kilgore Trout of *Galápagos* is a far cry from the Trout of, say, *God Bless You, Mr. Rosewater*, whose last word is "Joy." But as Vonnegut has admitted, his old recurrent character is "different in every book."[4]

If the ghost of Leon Trout never comes fully to life as a character in *Galápagos*, neither do the "living" characters he observes. At one point Leon describes all the major figures in the novel as "nature's experiment" with various abstract qualities: Wait is greed, Captain von Kleist is "ill-founded self-confidence," MacIntosh the entrepreneur is heartlessness, and so on (82). This abstract, bloodless quality is precisely the problem with the novel: its characters never strike the reader as much more than Vonnegut's way of sketching out his scenario for the deevolution of the human race.

Early in *Galápagos* Vonnegut seems to have had more ambitious plans, at least in Wait's case. Vonnegut said that he took the name James Wait from Joseph Conrad's story "The Nigger of the *Narcissus*."[5] But the more important precursor for Vonnegut in *Galápagos* is not Conrad but another great writer of sea stories— Herman Melville. One of the ships in Vonnegut's book is the *Omoo*, the title of one of Melville's early novels. This detail strongly suggests that Vonnegut was thinking of Melville as he wrote *Galápagos*. And the Melville novel he was thinking of most often was almost certainly *The Confidence Man*, which features a James Wait–like con artist who dupes people on board a ship. But while Melville built his character into a complex symbol for such various flawed embodiments of the American character as the salesman, the charismatic preacher, and the secular proponent of positive thinking (Ralph Waldo Emerson, to be specific), Vonnegut's James Wait simply fades from center stage as *Galápagos* progresses. Literally and symbolically, Vonnegut does not take him very far. He ends up dying of a heart attack in Mary Hepburn's arms just after marrying her en route to the Galápagos.

Admittedly, Vonnegut may have made the characters of his most scientific novel seem shadowy and insignificant on purpose. He may have wanted to suggest that the infinite ironies, ambiguities, and enigmas of "big-brained" human experience may one day simply become excess baggage in an overpopulated, dynamic ecosystem where change is the only constant. When self-conscious, highly intelligent humans existed, Vonnegut argues from his million-year perspective, they used those abilities to lie, to change their identities to suit the occasion, even to destroy themselves with highly complex weapons. If intelligence becomes a threat to survival, Vonnegut sensibly argues, then humans who become less intelligent will be more likely to survive.

Thus *Galápagos* is a sort of strange reversal of the

account of man's fall in the Bible. In the biblical story Adam and Eve ate the fruit of the tree of knowledge against God's prohibition, and so became self-conscious, capable of evil, and doomed to a life of hard work, pain, and death outside Eden's boundaries. In *Galápagos* man in effect reverses that decision to become knowledgeable and so regains a blissful but animal existence as a furry, web-footed, fish-eating mammal. When Captain von Kleist throws a computer called Mandarax (invented by the Japanese computer whiz) into the ocean—a machine that can translate most of the world's languages and call up quotations from famous writers on any subject—he is unconsciously carrying out man's symbolic rejection of higher thought in favor of a simpler existence. Mary Hepburn meets her end when she, as a schoolteacher and lover of knowledge, tries to save the device, only to be eaten along with it and von Kleist himself by a great white shark. Vonnegut's point is clear: intelligence has no special claim to ensuring survival on earth. Sharks, relatively simple eating machines, have survived much longer than man with virtually no evolutionary changes. No changes are needed when the organism perfectly fits the environment. Hyperintelligent man, on the other hand, may simply prove to be a flash in the evolutionary pan—one of nature's experiments that worked for a short while but then began to look more like fool's gold.

But finally Vonnegut's aim in *Galápagos* is less grim.

GALÁPAGOS

The novel is like Jonathan Swift's "A Modest Proposal" in being the opposite of what it initially appears. Vonnegut no more hopes for the extinction of human intelligence than Swift wanted the Irish literally to sell their children to the English to eat. At various points in the novel Vonnegut's voice breaks through his persona of Leon Trout, and the reader senses that *Galápagos* is meant as a warning, not an expression of scientific indifference to human fate. No book of purely objective evolutionary biology, for example, would begin with *Galápagos*'s epigraph from the diary of Anne Frank, the young Jewish girl who met her death in a Nazi concentration camp: "In spite of everything, I still believe people are really good at heart." Vonnegut is anything but neutral when he describes the terrible ecological effects of many of MacIntosh's corporate projects, or when he has his narrator describe the horrors of the Vietnam war. At one point, when Leon is considering entering the blue tunnel to the afterlife at the urging of his father, he wonders, "Have I at last exhausted my curiosity as to what life is all about?" (251–52). While *Galápagos* at times seems to suggest that its author might answer "yes" to that question, he finally answers quite differently. Near the end of the novel Leon admits that living, or at least observing, the purely animal existence of man simply will not suffice for him: "Nothing ever happens around here anymore that I haven't seen or heard so many times before. Nobody, surely, is going to write

Beethoven's Ninth Symphony—or tell a lie, or start a Third World War. Mother was right: Even in the darkest times, there really was hope for humankind" (259). On the Galápagos Islands of A.D. 1,000,000 there are no Nazi death camps, but no Beethoven, either. Man has lost the capacity to make war on himself, but also to create art, recognize his own mortality, wonder about his place in the cosmos, or know what it is to feel hope. So Leon awaits the reappearance of the blue tunnel, knowing by the novel's end that there is nothing left on earth worth staying around for.

Galápagos is a striking, somber book whose seeming flaws—sketchy characterization, emotional chilliness, and failure to deliver a second half that satisfies the expectations raised in its first half—actually contribute to its theme. Sounding like the literary critical advocates of deconstruction, Vonnegut uses the language of the novel to undermine its own ground, suggesting that the complexities of human self-consciousness have meaning only in relation to each other, and little or no relation to events outside themselves. Galápagos uses intelligence to undercut intelligence, language to undercut language. Like The Confidence Man, it is an indictment of superficial American optimism and the universal human tendency to anthropomorphize the universe. Galápagos is a hard novel to like, but an impossible one to dismiss.

Bluebeard

Bluebeard (1987), Vonnegut's most recent novel to
date, at first seems as though it could hardly be more
different from *Galápagos* in terms of tone, subject matter, or theme. Unlike its predecessor it is realistic rather
than fanciful. *Galápagos* is chillingly impersonal and pessimistic about the long-term survival of humanity; *Bluebeard* is an intimate account of the emotional lives of its
characters that concludes with a rarity in Vonnegut's
work—a happy ending. The novel's last words, in fact,
spoken by its narrator, are unequivocally upbeat: "Oh,
happy Rabo Karabekian." While *Galápagos* and *Bluebeard*
are not as dissimilar as they might seem, the tensions
between them reveal much about the central preoccupations and conflicts of Vonnegut's fictional career—issues such as the increasingly autobiographical nature
of his work, his changing notion of sexual roles in the
postmodern world, and his sense of his worth as an
artist. In addition to these serious themes *Bluebeard* contains all the humor and inventiveness one expects in a
Vonnegut novel, as well as an extra measure of emotional warmth; moreover, Vonnegut succeeds in weav-
ing all these diverse strands into his richest fictional
tapestry since *Slaughterhouse-Five*.

Bluebeard is the autobiography of Rabo Karabekian,
who in the present of the novel (1987) is seventy-one
years old. Like most of Vonnegut's protagonists Rabo

has been most profoundly affected by two things: his unhappy parents and his participation in World War II. His parents survived the massacre of most of their fellow Armenians by the Turks during World War I, fled Turkey to Cairo, then made their way to San Ignacio, California, where Rabo was born. Their pessimism is the understandable result of their seeing most of their countrymen slaughtered and of later being tricked out of all their money by a fellow Armenian in Cairo. Rabo's mother had played dead in a pile of corpses during the massacre, and had found jewels spilling out of the mouth of one of the bodies. In Cairo, Vartan Mamigorian had swindled her and Rabo's father out of the jewels by selling them a fake deed to a house in San Ignacio, where there was supposedly a thriving Armenian community. When the Karabekians arrive to find no house and no Armenian community, Rabo's father gives up on life, abandoning his scholarly interests in favor of cobbling. Then the Depression wipes out what little remains of his parents' money and hopes.

Out of these unpromising beginnings Rabo manages to make his way in the world, finally ending up as a wealthy man with an ocean-front estate on Long Island and one of the most valuable collections of Abstract Expressionist paintings in the world. Getting his start by writing to the famous illustrator Dan Gregory (Gregory's mistress actually answers the letters), Rabo soon becomes Gregory's artistic apprentice in New York City during the Depression. Modeled on Norman Rockwell

in terms of his middlebrow artistic sensibility and popularity, Gregory turns out to be quite different in terms
of his character. While Vonnegut has written that his
novels never contain a villain, this sadistic, sexist ad-
mirer of Mussolini surely is an exception. He kicks Rabo
out when he sees him coming out of a museum with
Marilee Kemp, his mistress, leaving Rabo once again to
make his way alone in the world.

After struggling through the Depression, Rabo goes
to war and persuades his commanding officer to form a
special camouflage unit manned by himself and other
artists. They constitute one of the artificial families that
frequently appear in Vonnegut's work. When pressed
into actual combat during the Battle of the Bulge, Rabo
loses an eye to a bullet and is captured by the Germans.
He is released at the end of the war to find himself in a
valley with thousands of soldiers, prisoners, and civilians of all nationalities. It is a scene he, like Vonnegut
himself, never forgets.

After the war Rabo marries, has two sons, falls in
with a crowd of painters (actual historical figures like
Jackson Pollock and Mark Rothko and fictional ones like
Terry Kitchen), begins to try his own hand at abstract
painting, then sees his marriage break up because he
won't get a steady job. He eventually suffers having his
painter friends kill themselves one by one, and his own
paintings self-destruct because he did them in a new
but defective paint. Alone and scorned by the art world,
he retreats to his ocean-front estate (the legacy of his

UNDERSTANDING KURT VONNEGUT

second wife, who died of heart failure) and becomes a virtual hermit—a "museum guard" for his art collection. At the opening of the book Rabo reveals that this state of death-in-life has been ended by the appearance of Circe Berman—a sexy, forty-three-year-old widow who shows up on his private beach one day and promptly asks him to "tell me how your parents died."[6] Rabo ends up inviting her to his house for dinner, and then into his life. In short order she has him feeling things intensely again and writing his autobiography—a process by which he recollects all the painful events of his past in order to do what psychologists call the "sorrow work" of getting over them and at last healing himself emotionally.

From the uncharacteristically explicit scene in which Rabo and Marilee Kemp make love, to Rabo's remarks about the interrelationship between art and eros, to the complex, highly erotic but unconsummated relationship between Rabo and Circe, Vonnegut has clearly written his most sexually charged fiction in *Bluebeard*. While Vonnegut has not exclusively avoided the subject in his novels (one thinks of Howard Campbell's erotic joy with his wife Helga in *Mother Night*), he has tended to downplay sexuality in favor of other issues. As he remarked in an interview,

There's a mechanical reason for avoiding adult sexual love in a book. The minute you introduce that element the reader's not going to want to hear anything more

BLUEBEARD

about the factory system or about what it's like to be a parachutist. He's going to want to hear about the guy getting the girl and this is a terrible distraction unless you're really going to deal flat out with the sexual theme.[7]

It would be fair to call *Bluebeard* a profeminist novel, since women and their struggles in a patriarchal world figure so importantly in it, and because women finally emerge as generally morally superior to men. Having grown up long before the feminist movement, Vonnegut has profoundly altered his attitudes toward women in the course of his career. His portraits of women range all the way from the stereotypically vapid 1950s housewife Anita Proteus in *Player Piano* to the independent, aggressive, financially capable, intellectually secure Marilee Kemp and Circe Berman of *Bluebeard*. There is an enormous distance between those characters. In the 1980s Vonnegut came to the conclusion that men have caused most of the horrors of the twentieth century and that, as the title of Rabo Karabekian's last painting proclaims, "Now It's the Women's Turn." He drives home the point in a scene in which Rabo and Marilee have a reunion in Florence after the war. She is now a wealthy countess, and a widow. Expecting a renewal of their sexual relationship, Rabo arrives at her palazzo to discover that because of her disgust with the war she has created a world without men. Living with her are women abused by their husbands, as she had been by Dan Gregory (he had pushed her down a flight of stairs upon discovering she had stolen some of his art supplies to send to Rabo), and those injured in the fighting. One of these women has an artificial leg, and Marilee explains that she lost it while

carrying two precious eggs to a neighbor who had given birth to a baby the night before. She stepped on a mine. We don't know what army was responsible. We do know the sex. Only a male would design and bury a device that ingenious. . . .

Women are so useless and unimaginative, aren't they? All they ever think of planting in the dirt is the seed of something beautiful or edible (224–25).

And *Bluebeard* as a whole acknowledges that women do much more nurturing of life than destroying of it. Even in leaving Rabo his first wife was doing what she thought best for their two sons. Marilee's all-female world functions as an emotional shelter for all the psychologically and physically wounded women living there. Finally, Circe transforms Rabo's sterile estate into a living place. Because of her contagious vitality he is writing, as is his friend Paul Slazinger, and Allison the cook is pregnant. Before Circe's appearance Allison had found Rabo so cold that having a child in those emotional surroundings seemed ridiculous. The title *Bluebeard* refers to the story of a brutal man who kept murdering his wives and putting their bodies in a room he forbade his new wife to enter. The women of the novel reverse that image, filling their rooms with life rather than death, inviting all inside rather than forbidding their entry. In *Bluebeard* it is indeed the women's turn.

If the novel is structured on the opposition of the sexes, it is also formed out of several other oppositions: war versus peace, loneliness versus community, and a nonrepresentational versus a representational aesthetic of painting—and by extension of art in general. In the case of the last pair representational art seems to win the day, but not in an oversimplified way. Rabo has clearly come to favor nonrepresentational art despite his beginnings with Dan Gregory. He is used to having all visitors to his collection of abstract paintings ask the inevitable question: "What are these pictures supposed to *mean*?" Rabo loves these paintings precisely because they are "about absolutely nothing but themselves" (8). As he explains late in the book to Circe, "The whole magical thing about our painting, Mrs. Berman, and this was old stuff in music, but it was brand new in painting: it was pure *essence of human wonder*" (294). Art like Dan Gregory's, while technically proficient, is always second-rate because it falsifies and sentimentalizes reality. His paintings always freeze "great moments" like those in Norman Rockwell's work, but they fail "to indicate somehow that time was liquid, that one moment was no more important than any other, and that all moments quickly run away." Gregory could never hope to achieve the highest of aesthetic effects, those "achieved by the best of the Abstract Expressionists, in the paintings which have greatness." In such paintings, Rabo explains, "birth and death are always there" (84)—not just some "frozen moment" highlighting one or the other but usually the former.

Yet the novel will not allow the simple notion that representational art is always inferior to abstract art. Circe herself is decidedly a representational artist. Her twenty-one best-selling novels for adolescents reveal detailed field research on the way contemporary teenagers act and think. She is in fact on Long Island to research a book on poor teens who try to make it into the circles of their affluent peers. Circe hates Rabo's collection of art, remarking of a Jackson Pollock that it should be "an advertisement for a hangover remedy or seasick pills" (24). After tricking Rabo into visiting New York City for the first time in years, she repaints his oyster-white walls and replaces his paintings with Victorian chromos of little girls on swings. When Rabo confronts Circe, she justifies herself by rightly observing that "I brought you back to life" (127).

Circe's aesthetic is that art must first and foremost communicate with an audience. And the way she believes a writer does that is to tell a meaningful story simply, without condescension, as though speaking to one person—in her case, to her dead husband. Vonnegut has said much the same thing in several interviews—that he is in a sense still writing for his sister Alice, who died in 1958 of cancer. But Rabo isn't really so far from Circe anyway in terms of aesthetics. Even in his abstract phase, he confesses, "I couldn't help seeing stories in my own compositions" (211). Still, *Bluebeard* shows Vonnegut's respect for artists who follow their own vision, even if it leads them into esoteric forms unlikely to be understood by the masses.

In his latest novel, as in all his later fiction, Vonnegut is struggling with highly autobiographical matters, both personal and professional. Rabo is a painter and only very late a writer, but his career closely parallels Vonnegut's. His early representational period corresponds to his creator's start in journalism, in which the first rule is simply to get the facts straight. Vonnegut learned those lessons well when working on his high school and college newspapers. Rabo's nonrepresentational period resembles Vonnegut's experimental fiction, beginning with *Cat's Cradle* and progressing through *Slaughterhouse-Five* and finally ending with the antinovel *Breakfast of Champions*. Like Rabo, Vonnegut began his experimental phase in obscurity, but by the end of it was rich and famous, selling his books by the millions, just as Rabo would receive millions for his Abstract Expressionist paintings. Moreover, Rabo's dismay over the fact that his work in the period self-destructed because of the defective paint he used, and his even greater dismay when he realized he wasn't much of an abstract artist anyway, surely reflect Vonnegut's self-doubts about his work in the 1970s. Before his return to "representational" fiction in the 1980s Vonnegut must have feared that he would go down in literary history as Rabo had in art history—as a curious but decidedly minor footnote. *Bluebeard,* like Vonnegut's career, however, has a great last phase that redeems the artist by taking him back to his beginnings—to his childhood experiences with despairing parents and to his early realistic modes of self-expression. Like Hemingway's *The Old Man and the Sea*, in which Hemingway talked about his writing in terms of fishing, Bluebeard is a fictionalized autobiography of a writer's career—his summation of his strengths, weaknesses, and his treatment by his public and the critics.

This latter aspect of the novel becomes clear when Rabo at last shows Circe the painting he has kept hidden, locked away since he painted it just after his second wife died. He at first plans to let the potato barn be opened only after his death, because, as he tells Circe, "I don't want to be around when people say whether it is any good or not" (279). Speaking almost directly to the reader about the critical disapproval of him as merely a popular writer, Vonnegut has Rabo say, after he changes his mind and shows Circe and later the public his last work,

No solemn critic has yet appeared. . . . I will tell the first critic to show up, if one ever comes, and one may never come, since the whatchamacallit is so exciting to the common people:

"It isn't a painting at all! It's a tourist attraction! It's a World's Fair! It's a Disneyland!" (283).

Vonnegut has always faced the charge from some critics that his work is precisely like Disneyland—high tech, enormously popular, but ultimately founded on a cartoon aesthetic. But as Rabo quickly points out of his painting, if Vonnegut's writing is the literary equivalent of Disneyland, "It is a gruesome Disneyland. Nobody is cute there" (283). And how could there be Disneyland without cuteness? Rabo's final painting, like Vonnegut's writing, does not please its audience in a facile way—by banishing death and despair as Disneyland does—but by dealing with them and the grand themes that move every human heart: the horrors of war, the persistence of love despite those horrors, the sense of wonder at merely being alive in our profoundly mysterious cosmos.

Rabo proves he is no Bluebeard when he finally opens up his potato barn. Contrary to Vonnegut's almost career-long tendency to intentionally diffuse suspense by giving away the endings of his novels in chapter 1, he goes back to traditional storytelling here by offering tantalizing hints about his secret all through the book. Part of the success of *Bluebeard* is the simple satisfaction it offers at the end to the reader, who "sees" the painting with the same sense of wonder and surprise as Circe. Like a child being led to a present, Circe lets Rabo orchestrate her viewing of "Now It's the Women's Turn":

She closed her eyes, and she followed me as unre- sistingly as a toy balloon.
    When we were in the middle, with thirty-two feet of the painting extending to either side, I told her to open her eyes again.
    We were standing on the rim of a beautiful green valley in the springtime. By actual count, there were five thousand, two hundred and nineteen people on the rim with us or down below. The largest person was the size of a cigarette, and the smallest a flyspeck. . . . The picture was so realistic that it might have been a photo- graph.
    "Where are we?" said Circe Berman.
    "Where I was," I said, "when the sun came up the day the Second World War ended in Europe (280–81).

Circe is profoundly moved by Rabo's epic canvas, by the combination of pathos and joy that she sees there. In his representational work Rabo has been able to do what he never could in his abstract paintings: put birth and death side by side in a great moment that still sug- gests that time is "liquid." Years earlier, when he had taken art classes at New York University, a teacher had denigrated Rabo's work because while technically profi- cient he was "a man without passion" who seemed to have "absolutely nothing which he is desperate to talk about" (190). But after years of emotional sterility Rabo at last finds a profound subject to go with his craftsmanship and release his soul—the great passion of Vonnegut himself, World War II.

Rabo leaves the world one last great painting; likewise, Vonnegut leaves the novel *Bluebeard*, even while suggesting through the subject matter of Rabo's painting that the greatest work in the potato barn of his fiction is still *Slaughterhouse-Five*. Both novels end with the same scene: a valley filled with people of all nationalities who have somehow survived the worst event in history but who are about to begin again. Early in *Bluebeard* Circe had complained that Rabo had "never got past the Great Depression and World War Two" (125). But making sense out of traumatic events by shaping them into art *is* getting past them, and learning to trust others again is an essential part of that process. Vonnegut chose as his epigraph to *Bluebeard* a line from a letter his son Mark wrote to him: "We are here to help each other get through this thing, whatever it is." Like Rabo Karabekian, Vonnegut has come through the tragedies of this century, in his life and in his art.

Notes

1. *Galápagos* (New York: Delacorte/Lawrence, 1985) 270. Subsequent references are noted parenthetically.

UNDERSTANDING KURT VONNEGUT

2. *Conversations with Kurt Vonnegut*, ed. William Rodney Allen (Jackson: University Press of Mississippi, 1988) 291. Hereafter *CKV*.

3. *CKV* 291.

4. *CKV* 263.

5. *CKV* 257.

6. *Bluebeard* (New York: Delacorte, 1987) 13. Subsequent references are noted parenthetically.

7. *CKV* 53.

CONCLUSION

After the listing of his fifteen major books opposite the title page of *Bluebeard*, Vonnegut adds a paren-
thetical remark: "Enough! Enough!" Just after *Bluebeard*
was published, Paul Smith and I asked Vonnegut
whether that aside suggested he planned to retire from
writing fiction. His reply would probably strike a re-
sponsive chord in many a writer: "No. I'd like to,
though. It's a hell of a lot of work. You're doing it all
by yourself."[1] Vonnegut will probably write more novels, but as a man approaching seventy he has already
produced most of the work he will leave to the world.
At least five of his novels—*Mother Night, Cat's Cradle,
Slaughterhouse-Five, Jailbird,* and *Bluebeard*—seem likely
to endure for a long time in our collective consciousness. *Slaughterhouse-Five* should become a part of the
American literary canon—if a *granfalloon* like "canon" is
an appropriate frame of reference for that novel.

The question of ranking Vonnegut's work has been
a constant concern since the first reviews of his novels
began appearing in the 1960s. If for no other reason, his

career will be studied as an ideal reflection of the history of popular and critical taste in the second half of this century. Joe David Bellamy called Vonnegut "the thinking man's pop writer."[2] One could add that he is also the thinking woman's, especially in his profeminist novels of the 1980s. The fact is that Vonnegut has responded thoughtfully to the major cultural changes of several decades—from feminism back through the Reagan era and the scandal-plagued 1970s to the youth movement and the Vietnam war, on back to the consumer culture of the 1950s and to World War II, and finally to the Depression. Because Vonnegut's experiences are those of so many Americans, Klinkowitz thinks that his life "becomes a mythology for America itself, which is the principal reason why Vonnegut is so popular."[3]

There is by now no need to prove that Vonnegut should be accepted as an important American writer: he already has been. As he says in an interview, "Allen Ginsberg and I both got elected to the National Institute of Arts and Letters and *Newsweek* asked me how I felt about two such freaks getting into such an august organization. I said, 'If we aren't the establishment, I don't know who is.'"[4] As for lasting forever as a literary monument, Vonnegut is typically irreverent: "When I think of my own death, I don't console myself with the idea that my descendants and my books all will live on. Anybody with any sense knows that the whole Solar System will go up like a celluloid collar by-and-by."[5] A

CONCLUSION

typically offbeat Vonnegut image combining the futuristic and the slightly antiquated but homey—our little
corner of the universe burning up like a turn-of-the-
century shirt collar. Until that conflagration, that cosmic
Dresden, Vonnegut's books will be worth reading.

Notes

1. *Conversations with Kurt Vonnegut*, ed. William Rodney Allen
(Jackson: University Press of Mississippi, 1988) 291. Hereafter *CKV*.

2. Joe David Bellamy, "Vonnegut for President," *The Vonnegut
Statement*, ed. Jerome Klinkowitz and John Somer (New York: De-
lacorte/Lawrence, 1973) 81.

3. Jerome Klinkowitz, "Vonnegut in America," *Vonnegut in America*, ed. Klinkowitz and Donald L. Lawler (New York: Delacorte/Law-
rence, 1977) 8.

4. *CKV* 107.

5. *CKV* 235.

BIBLIOGRAPHY

Works by Kurt Vonnegut
Novels

Player Piano. New York: Scribner's, 1952; London: Macmillan, 1953. (New York: Delacorte/Lawrence, 1971.)

The Sirens of Titan. New York: Dell, 1959; London, Gollancz, 1962. (New York: Delacorte/Lawrence, 1971.)

Mother Night. Greenwich, CT: Fawcett, 1962; London: Jonathan Cape, 1968. (New York: Harper, 1966.) (New York: Delacorte/Lawrence, 1971.)

Cat's Cradle. New York: Holt, Rinehart, 1963; London: Gollancz, 1963. (New York: Delacorte/Lawrence, 1971.)

God Bless You, Mr. Rosewater. New York: Holt, Rinehart, 1965; London: Jonathan Cape, 1965. (New York: Delacorte/Lawrence, 1971.)

Slaughterhouse-Five. New York: Delacorte/Lawrence, 1969; London: Jonathan Cape, 1970.

Breakfast of Champions. New York: Delacorte/Lawrence, 1973; London: Granada, 1974.

Slapstick. New York: Delacorte/Lawrence, 1976; London: Jonathan Cape, 1976.

Jailbird. New York: Delacorte/Lawrence, 1979; London: Jonathan Cape, 1979.

Deadeye Dick. New York: Delacorte/Lawrence, 1982; London: Jonathan Cape, 1983.

Galápagos. New York: Delacorte/Lawrence, 1985; London: Jonathan Cape, 1985.

Bluebeard. New York: Delacorte, 1987; London: Jonathan Cape, 1987.

Short Story Collections

Canary in a Cat House. Greenwich, CT: Fawcett, 1961.

Welcome to the Monkey House. New York: Delacorte/Lawrence, 1968; London: Jonathan Cape, 1969.

177

BIBLIOGRAPHY

Drama

Happy Birthday, Wanda June. New York: Delacorte/Lawrence, 1970; London: Jonathan Cape, 1972.

Screenplay for Television

Between Time and Timbuktu. New York: Delacorte/Lawrence, 1972; London: Granada, 1975.

Children's Fiction

Sun Moon Star. New York: Harper, 1980; London: Hutchinson, 1980.

Essays

Wampeters, Foma, and Granfalloons. New York: Delacorte/Lawrence, 1974; London: Jonathan Cape, 1975.

Palm Sunday. New York: Delacorte/Lawrence, 1981; London: Jonathan Cape, 1982.

Two Essays: Nothing Is Lost Save Honor. Jackson, MS: Nouveau Press, 1984.

Political Pamphlets

Fates Worse than Death. Nottingham, England: Russell Press, 1982.

Selected Uncollected Essays

"Science Fiction." *New York Times Book Review* 5 Sept. 1965: 2.

"Reading Your Own." *New York Times Book Review* 4 June 1967: 6.

"The High Cost of Fame." *Playboy* Jan. 1971: 124.

"Vonnegut on Trout." *Fantasy and Science Fiction* 48 (1975): 158.

"New York: Who Needs It?" *Harper's* 3 Aug. 1975: 3.

"A Reluctant Big Shot." *Nation* 7 Mar. 1981: 282–83.

"A Truly Modern Hero." *Psychology Today* Aug. 1981: 9–10.

"Jack the Dripper." *Esquire* Dec. 1983: 549–54.

"The Worst Addiction of Them All." *Nation* 31 Dec.–7 Jan. 1984: 681, 698.

BIBLIOGRAPHY

"The Idea Killers." *Playboy* Jan. 1984: 122, 260, 262.
"Imagine the Worst." *Mother Jones* 26 Oct. 1984.

Selected Works About Vonnegut
Interviews
Allen, William Rodney, ed. *Conversations with Kurt Vonnegut.* Jackson: University Press of Mississippi, 1988. Twenty-one of the most important interviews with Vonnegut. Includes a previously unpublished interview with the editor.
Uncollected Interviews
Banks, Ann. "Symposium Sidelights." *Novel* 3 (1970): 208–11.
Bosworth, Patricia. "To Vonnegut, the Hero Is the Man Who Refuses to Kill." *New York Times* 25 Oct. 1970: sec. 2, 5.
Cargas, Harry James. "Are There Things a Novelist Shouldn't Joke About?" *Christian Century* 24 Nov. 1976: 1048–50.
Cook, Bruce. "When Kurt Vonnegut Talks—and He Does—the Young All Tune In." *National Observer* 12 Oct. 1970: 2.
Diskey, Jay A. "Vonnegut Cradles His Fiction in Imagination and Experience." *Indiana Daily Student* 5 Oct. 1983: 1, 6.
Eckholt, Larry. "Vonnegut Vows to Survive Critics." *Des Moines Register* 2 Apr. 1977: 1B.
Friedenreich, Kenneth. "Kurt Vonnegut: The PR Man Turned Novelist." *Newsday* 11 Aug. 1975.
Horwitz, Carey. "An Interview with Kurt Vonnegut, Jr." *Library Journal* 15 Apr. 1973: 1311.
Klinkowitz, Jerome. "Lonesome No More: Interview with Kurt Vonnegut." *Washington Post World* 2 Sept. 1979: 7.
Mahoney, Lawrence. "Poison Their Minds with Humanity." *Tropic: The Miami Herald Sunday Magazine* 24 Jan. 1971: 8–10, 13, 44.

180

BIBLIOGRAPHY

Merryman, Kathleen. "Vonnegut Blasts America's Lack of Idealism." *Tacoma News Tribune* 26 Apr. 1985: C10.

Romine, Dannye. "Listening to Kurt Vonnegut, Higgledly-Piggledly." *Charlotte Observer-Sun* 18 Feb. 1979: 1F, 8F.

Thomas, Phil. "Growing Sales Puzzle Writer." *Ann Arbor News* 12 Dec. 1971: 41.

Wolf, William. "Kurt Vonnegut: Still Dreaming of Imaginary Worlds." *Insight: Sunday Magazine of the Milwaukee Journal* 28 Feb. 1972: 12–18.

Books

Broer, Lawrence R. *Sanity Plea: Schizophrenia in the Novels of Kurt Vonnegut.* Ann Arbor: UMI, 1989.

Giannone, Richard. *Vonnegut: A Preface to His Novels.* Port Washington, NY: Kennikat Press, 1977. A sophisticated study tracing biblical and other sources and analyzing the formal innovations that come to fruition in *Slaughterhouse-Five*.

Goldsmith, David. *Kurt Vonnegut: Fantasist of Fire and Ice,* Bowling Green, OH: Bowling Green University Popular Press, 1972. Emphasis on messiah figures and on Vonnegut's metaphysical skepticism.

Klinkowitz, Jerome. *Kurt Vonnegut.* New York: Methuen, 1982. Excellent short treatment of Vonnegut's work through *Jailbird*.

Lundquist, James. *Kurt Vonnegut.* New York: Ungar, 1976. A competent if unspectacular treatment of Vonnegut as a celebrator of middle-class life despite his outlandish subject matter.

Mayo, Clark. *Kurt Vonnegut: The Gospel from Outer Space.* San Bernardino: R. Reginald/Borgo Press, 1977. An overly enthusiastic treatment that contains some useful insights.

BIBLIOGRAPHY

Reed, Peter J. *Kurt Vonnegut, Jr.* New York: Warner, 1972. A solid, detailed treatment of Vonnegut's themes and techniques through *Slaughterhouse-Five.*

Schatt, Stanley. *Kurt Vonnegut, Jr.* Boston: Twayne, 1976. A study of mixed results emphasizing Vonnegut's messiah figures.

Short, Robert. *Something to Believe In: Is Kurt Vonnegut the Exorcist of Jesus Christ Superstar?* New York: Harper, 1978. A study of limited usefulness and depth.

Collections of Essays

Klinkowitz, Jerome, and John Somer, eds. *The Vonnegut Statement.* New York: Delacorte/Lawrence, 1973. An indispensable collection of early essays on Vonnegut by critics and friends.

Klinkowitz, Jerome, and Donald L. Lawler, eds. *Vonnegut in America.* New York: Delacorte/Lawrence, 1977. Many insightful essays on Vonnegut by his leading critics.

Books That Discuss Vonnegut

Aldiss, Brian W. *Billion Year Spree: The True History of Science Fiction.* Garden City, NY: Doubleday, 1973. 258, 278–79, 313–16.

Berger, Harold L. *Science Fiction and the New Dark Age.* Bowling Green, OH: Bowling Green University Popular Press, 1976. ix, 9, 17–19, 20, 22, 25, 37, 65, 69, 77, 123, 124, 215n.

Blair, John G. *The Confidence Man in Modern Fiction.* New York: Harper, 1979. 14, 15, 24, 98, 99–111, 113, 132–36, 139.

Broer, Lawrence. "Pilgrim's Progress: Is Kurt Vonnegut, Jr., Winning His War with Machines?" *Clockwork Worlds: Mechanized Environments in Science Fiction,* ed. Richard D. Erlich and Thomas P. Dunn. Westport, CT: Greenwood Press, 1983. 137–61.

182

BIBLIOGRAPHY

Bryant, Jerry H. *The Open Decision*. New York: Free Press, 1970. 303–24.

Crichton, Michael. *"Slaughterhouse-Five." The Critic as Artist: Essays on Books, 1920–1970*, ed. Gilbert A. Harrison. New York: Liveright, 1972. 100–07.

Harris, Charles B. *Contemporary American Novelists of the Absurd*. New Haven: College and University Press, 1971. 51–75.

Hipkiss, Robert A. *The American Absurd: Pynchon, Vonnegut, and Barth*. Port Washington, NY: Associated Faculty Press, 1984. 43–73.

Jones, Peter G. *War and the Novelist*. Columbia: University of Missouri Press, 1976. 2, 203–29, 234–35.

Kennard, Jean. *Number and Nightmare: Forms of Fantasy in Contemporary Literature*. Hamden, CT: Archon Books/Shoe String Press, 1975. 101–28, 131–33, 203–04.

Nelson, Gerald B. "Eliot Rosewater." *Ten Versions of America*. New York: Knopf, 1972. 61–76.

Pinsker, Sanford. "Fire and Ice: The Radical Cuteness of Kurt Vonnegut, Jr." *Between Two Worlds: The American Novel in the 1960's*. Troy, NY: Whitston, 1980. 1–19.

Sadler, Frank. "Time and the Structure of Reality." *The Unified Ring: Narrative Art and the Science-Fiction Novel*. Ann Arbor: UMI Research Press, 1984. 73–89.

Scholes, Robert. "Fabulation and Satire." *The Fabulators*. New York: Oxford University Press, 1967. 35–55.

Stableford, Brian M. "Locked in the Slaughterhouse: The Novels of Kurt Vonnegut." *Essays on Six Science Fiction Authors*. San Bernardino: R. Reginald/Borgo Press, 1981. 15–23.

Tanner, Tony. *City of Words*. New York: Harper, 1971. 181–201.

BIBLIOGRAPHY

Vanderbilt, Kermit. "Kurt Vonnegut's American Nightmares and Utopias." *The Utopian Vision: Seven Essays on the Quincentennial of Sir Thomas More.* San Diego: San Diego State University Press, 1983. 137–73.

Warrick, Patricia S. *The Cybernetic Imagination in Science Fiction.* Cambridge: MIT Press, 1980. 89, 125, 134–39.

Wright, Moorhead. "The Existential Adventurer and War: Three Case Studies from American Fiction." *American Thinking about Peace and War,* ed. Ken Booth and Morhead Wright. New York: Barnes and Noble, 1978. 101–10.

Critical Articles

Berryman, Charles. "After the Fall: Kurt Vonnegut." *Critique* 26 (1985): 96–102. Good treatment of Vonnegut's post–*Slaughterhouse-Five* fiction.

Blackford, Russell. "The Definition of Love: Kurt Vonnegut's *Slapstick.*" *Science Fiction* July 1980: 208–28.

Bourjaily, Vance. "What Vonnegut Is and Isn't." *New York Times Book Review* 13 Aug. 1972: 3, 10.

Buck, Lynn. "Vonnegut's World of Comic Futility." *Studies in American Fiction* 3 (1975): 181–98.

Chabot, C. Barry. "*Slaughterhouse-Five* and the Comforts of Indifference." *Essays in Literature* 8 (1981): 45–51.

Clancy, L. J. "'If the Accident Will': The Novels of Kurt Vonnegut." *Meanjin Quarterly* 30 (1971): 37–45. Good early study recognizing the development of Vonnegut's work to the culmination of *Slaughterhouse-Five.*

Demott, Benjamin. "Vonnegut's Otherworldly Laughter." *Saturday Review* 1 May 1971: 29–32, 38. Treatment of the tension between realism and fantasy in Vonnegut's fiction.

Edelstein, Arnold. "*Slaughterhouse-Five:* Time Out of Joint." *College Literature* 1 (1974): 128–39.

BIBLIOGRAPHY

Fiedler, Leslie A. "The Divine Stupidity of Kurt Vonnegut." *Esquire* Sept. 1970: 195–97, 199–200, 202–04. Argues that Vonnegut is a popular novelist dealing in sentiment and myth, as opposed to an elite art novelist.

Friedman, Melvin J. "Dislocations of Setting and Word: Notes on American Fiction Since 1950." *Studies in American Fiction* 5 (1977): 79–98.

Greiner, Donald J. "Vonnegut's *Slaughterhouse-Five* and the Fiction of Atrocity." *Critique* 14. 3 (1973): 38–51.

Hansen, Arlen J. "The Celebration of Solipsism: A New Trend in American Fiction." *Modern Fiction Studies* 19 (1973): 5–15.

Hayman, David. "The Jolly Mix: Notes on Techniques, Style, and Decorum in *Slaughterhouse-Five*." *Summary* 1. 2 (1977): 44–50.

Hume, Kathryn. "The Heraclitan Cosmos of Kurt Vonnegut." *Papers on Language and Literature* 18 (1982): 208–24.

Irving, John. "Kurt Vonnegut and His Critics." *New Republic* 22 Sept. 1979: 41–49. Important defense of Vonnegut after the critical fallout over *Slapstick*.

Kazin, Alfred. "The War Novel from Mailer to Vonnegut." *Saturday Review* 6 Feb. 1971: 13–15, 36. Differences between Mailer's *The Naked and the Dead* and Heller's *Catch-22* and *Slaughterhouse-Five* indicate that Mailer's book looks backward, while the later two, written long after World War II, look forward to a possible next war.

Lawing, John V., Jr. "Kurt Vonnegut: Charming Nihilist." *Christianity Today* 14 Feb. 1979: 17–20, 22.

LeClair, Thomas. "Death and Black Humor." *Critique* 17.1 (1975): 5–40.

Leff, Leonard. "Science and Destruction in Vonnegut's *Cat's Cradle*." *Rectangle* 46 (1971): 28–32.

BIBLIOGRAPHY

Lessing, Doris. "Vonnegut's Responsibility." *New York Times Book Review* 4 Feb. 1973: 35. Praise of *Mother Night* for its exploration of difficult ethical questions.

Leverence, W. John. *"Cat's Cradle* and Traditional American Humor." *Journal of Popular Culture* 4 (1972): 955–63.

McGinnis, Wayne. "The Arbitrary Cycle of *Slaughterhouse-Five:* A Relation of Form to Theme." *Critique* 17.1 (1975): 55–68.

Matheson, T. J. " 'This Lousy Little Book': The Genesis and Development of *Slaughterhouse-Five* as Revealed in Chapter One." *Studies in the Novel* 16 (1984): 228–40.

Merrill, Robert. "Vonnegut's *Breakfast of Champions:* The Conversion of Heliogabalus." *Critique* 18.3 (1977): 99–108.

Nelson, Joyce. *"Slaughterhouse-Five:* Novel and Film." *Literature/Film Quarterly* 1 (1973): 149–53.

O'Sullivan, Maurice J., Jr. *"Slaughterhouse-Five:* Kurt Vonnegut's Anti-memoirs." *Essays in Literature* 3 (1976): 44–50.

Pütz, Manfred. "Imagination and Self-Definition." *Partisan Review* 44.2 (1977): 235–44.

Rackstraw, Loree. "Vonnegut Cosmos." *North American Review* 267 (1982): 63–67. Effective treatment of *Deadeye Dick.*

Rice, Susan. *"Slaughterhouse-Five:* A Viewer's Guide." *Media and Methods* Oct. 1972: 27–33.

Samuels, Charles Thomas. "Age of Vonnegut." *New Republic* 12 June 1971: 30–32. An account of the phenomenal rise to fame of Vonnegut as the result of his blending of sentimental themes with innovative techniques and modern skepticism.

Todd, Richard. *"Breakfast of Champions:* This Novel Contains More than Twice Your Daily Requirement of Irony." *Atlantic* May 1973: 105–09. Sees *Breakfast of Champions* as Vonnegut's dealing with the problems of fame.

BIBLIOGRAPHY

Wolfe, G. K. "Vonnegut and the Metaphor of Science Fiction: *The Sirens of Titan." Journal of Popular Culture* 4 (1972): 964–69.

Ziegfield, Richard E. "Kurt Vonnegut on Censorship and Moral Values." *Modern Fiction Studies* 26 (1980): 631–35.

Bibliography

Klinkowitz, Jerome; Julie Huffman-Klinkowitz, and Asa B. Pieratt, Jr., *Kurt Vonnegut: A Comprehensive Bibliography.* Hamden, CT: Archon Books, 1987. Primary and secondary. Supersedes all earlier bibliographies.

INDEX

AIDS, 151
American Civil Liberties Union, 7

Barth, John, 11, 51
Barthelme, Donald, 11
Bible, 84–88, 93, 113, 137, 138, 156
Brautigan, Richard, 11

Camus, Albert
Castro, Fidel, 62
Céline, Louis-Ferdinand, 94, 96; *Journey to the End of Night*, 96
Cicero, 80
Conrad, Joseph, 154; "The Nigger of the *Narcissus*," 154
Coover, Robert, 11
Crane, Stephen, 14

Dante, 106; *The Divine Comedy*, 106, 113
Darwin, Charles, 11, 67
Dickens, Charles, 15

Einstein, Albert, 42, 82, 131
Eliot, T. S., 146
Emerson, Ralph Waldo, 155

INDEX

INDEX

INDEX

INDEX

CPSIA information can be obtained at www.ICGtesting.com
Printed in the USA
245422LV00001B/4/P

9 781570 038860